Against All Odds

Inspirational true story of conquering cancer during pregnancy

AF541140

SUGAT GOPNARAYAN

An imprint of
Srishti Publishers & Distributors

Srishti Publishers & Distributors
A unit of AJR Publishing LLP
212A, Peacock Lane
Shahpur Jat, New Delhi – 110 049

editorial@srishtipublishers.com

First published by
Srishti Publishers & Distributors in 2023

Copyright © Sugat Gopnarayan, 2023

10 9 8 7 6 5 4 3 2 1

This is a work of non-fiction inspired from the author's true life events. The characters, places, organisations and events described in this book have been dramatized for storytelling purpose. The views expressed in the book are the author's own and are not intended to hurt the sentiments of any individual, community, sect or religion.

The author asserts the moral right to be identified as the author of this work.

All rights reserved.

No part of this publication may be reproduced, stored in a retrieval system, or transmitted, in any form or by any means, electronic, mechanical, photocopying, recording or otherwise, without the prior written permission of the Publishers.

Printed and bound in India

CONTENTS

ACKNOWLEDGEMENTS

A big thank you to Dr. Pranjali Gadgil, Dr. Tushar Patil, Dr. Jyoti Aggarwal, Dr. Vikas Kothavade, Dr. Prajakta Sabale, Dr. Jyoti Solanke, Dr. Sharada Umarani and Dr. Shrinivas Tambe.

You all are real life gods !

1

INTRODUCTION AND BACKGROUND

'*Yeh haseen waadiyaan, yeh khula aasmaan... aa gaye hum kaahaan, ae mere saajana...*'

These lines from a very popular song that I loved during my childhood were running through my mind and heart. I along with Deepika, the leading lady of this story, were sitting on a rock at 15,000 feet above sea level, at the edge of a snow-clad mountain in Sikkim, staring at the mighty Mount Kanchenjunga in front of us. It was a heavenly feeling – her sitting in front of me and my arms tightly wrapped around her. We were deeply immersed in the serene snow-white valley and the blue skies that stretched as far as the horizon. It felt as if time had stood still, and we were in a scene from a movie, far away from our busy lives spent running around, earning a livelihood. While sitting there, we were experiencing a bit of heaven, leaving our earthly worries behind.

This was in February 2020. Along with our college friends from Mumbai, our much awaited plan of going on a trip together, that had been years in the making, had finally materialised. Northeast of India was decided as the destination. So desperate we were for a trip, we headed towards it like an arrow left from a bow.

In our group, Pratique, Vishal and I had been in the same class in our engineering college when we passed out in 2010. We were in constant touch even after graduation. They were some of the very few friends with whom I managed to stay in regular touch. We shared a very strong bond, as we had been a part of many life events together, including our outings, relationships and weddings.

Deepika too had been a student in our college, but she was junior to me. Ours was a 'final-year guy fell for a first-year girl' type of love story. Since both of us hail from outside Mumbai, we had to stay in the college hostel. It was a common hostel building separating girls' and boys' areas with a partition. The canteen and hangout places were common for both. Those were the places where we first met and got to know each other. While we were just friends in college, we did not think that we could ever fall in love someday. We began chatting with each other more frequently after my graduation, and that was when we started getting to know each other better.

Chatting turned into calling, calling turned into overnight calling and overnight calling turned into being on call 24x7. Finally, we exchanged the three magical words on the 18th of December 2010. Purposely mentioning the dates, as this story can be very well plotted on a timeline till the last page.

The next date was the same 18th of December, but the year was 2015. The year we got married. After five years of being together, we decided to get married on the same date on which we had started our relationship. Now one would easily expect that since 2010 = relationship, 2015 = wedding, five years down the line in 2020, what next on the same date? Kid? Well, yes. Almost. Let's keep this on hold for now. We will deep dive into 2020 after a few pages.

For those five years, from 2010 to 2015, we lived in different cities. I shifted to Pune to begin my first job immediately after I passed out, and so began a long distance relationship for the two of us. We used to speak on the phone every single day, but could barely spend more than three to four weeks without a meeting. Mumbai, for those five years, was a monthly destination for me. Video calling was not so handy at that time. People had just recently started using Facebook and getting familiar with social media. There wasn't any WhatsApp for us until a few years later. In fact, till 2013, we just had that 'tring-tring' phone and SMS was the only means of chatting for us.

In March 2015, I got a chance for a six-month deputation in the United Kingdom. It was both a happy and sad occasion. While it was a promotional opportunity for me, it also meant a six-month ban on our meetings. My company sponsors spouse's expenses on a foreign trip, but she was not my spouse yet. That very moment I decided I would definitely take her along during my next trip. With great difficulty, we managed to spend those six months being apart, but luckily, by then, video calls had become a household thing. Those 'dooriyaan' definitely brought 'nazdikiyaan' in our relationship.

Six months later, by the time I was about to come back, we had a full-fledged plan of how we'd inform our parents and convince them to give us their go-ahead for our marriage. Interfaith weddings are still not preferred in India, but thankfully both our families were very supportive. Deepika's father was in the Indian Army, hence she had a very patriotic upbringing with no bias for any caste or religion. My family too did not have that bias. My mom is a big Bollywood fan and she always wished that I should marry a girl of my choice, irrespective of her faith. And when everyone agreed, I got married thrice! With the same girl, of course! Two weddings as per the faiths of each of our families, and one as per the faith of both of us – a court marriage.

Finally, after a wait of five long years, we began our life together in Pune. Deepika was keen on working, but for some reason, it didn't happen right away. Since childhood, she had a good understanding of leading a healthy lifestyle and eating well. I insisted that she pursue further studies in nutrition, her favourite field. She agreed for it happily, and a couple of years later, she became a certified nutritionist. A weird combination of engineer becoming a nutritionist, but that's what you end up with, when after doing something that is perceived as respectable, you finally listen to your heart.

By that time, our families, like every other Indian family, started asking us as to when we were giving them the 'good news'. But we were not ready yet. We wanted to travel together and enjoy our life as a couple first. So far, all we had was a short trip to Ooty.

I was keen on taking her on a foreign trip, and only after that, we would start a family. Ultimately, in December 2018, I got a chance to go to the UK once again. And this time, Deepika accompanied me as well. Those days, it was the trend to put a travel status on Facebook, especially when one was travelling abroad. I was no exception. As soon as we reached our departure gate, I grabbed my phone and punched in a nice travel status tagging Deepika.

We were to spend an entire month in the UK. On weekdays, I had to work, but we made the most of those four weekends, exploring and travelling as if there was no tomorrow. We knew that the next step would be planning our family. Coincidentally, our third anniversary was also coming up, and we got a chance to celebrate it in London that year. It was all like a dream come true.

After coming back from the UK, I had another dream to fulfill. This time it was related to my parents. Belonging to an average middle-class family, they were very curious about air travel, especially the flights I used to take. I wanted them to experience it as well. Also, my mother had a childhood dream of watching the Republic Day Parade in Delhi in person. So Deepika and I planned a trip to North India close to the 26th of January as a surprise for our parents. Somehow, I managed to get the passes for the parade, with help from Pratique. On the day our parents arrived in Pune, we surprised them with the announcement that we would be travelling to Delhi the next day, to see the parade live. My mom was very happy and excited. The next thing that I told her brought tears to her already happy eyes. I revealed that we were going by air and she would be embarking on her very first flight. Her joy was unimaginable, and it was a moment to cherish for life. A good five-day trip to North India followed in the first month of 2019.

A couple of months later, the focus was back on the question of us starting a family. Deepika, who had studied after marriage, hadn't begun working as yet. She wanted to work for at least a few months before getting pregnant. She missed being busy with her studies, and sitting idle at home was hitting her hard. She started looking for a job and thankfully got one quickly this time. We postponed the plan of having a baby by another six months.

In November 2019, it felt like it was finally time to start, but then another plan arrived on the cards. A trip with our friends which was long due, was finally taking shape. It was decided that we'd visit Northeast in February 2020. All the tickets got booked and hence once again, we couldn't give conception a try as it could hamper our trip plans. Pratique had been married for two years now. Deepika too was good friends with Pratique, Vishal and the other buddies of mine, as she knew all of them since our college days. We all spent some good time in local outings before our weddings as a friends group, but had never gone on a proper vacation. This was the time.

It was a wonderful trip, some moments of which I have described in the very first lines of this book. This time, after this trip, we indeed felt fulfilled from within. Deepika and I had shared some of the best times in those four years of marriage, with each other, with family, and with friends. Now that travel and trips were ticked off our list, we were ourselves looking forward to starting a family as soon as we headed back to Pune. We had taken our time, and had spent four years to live and fulfill our couple goals. It was worth it!

2

GOOD NEWS!

We were soon back in Pune, still hung over from the trip. At this time, the so far unknown entity coronavirus was spreading havoc across the western world, but India was yet to feel the brunt. We were very fortunate that we managed the air travel without any hitches, and could enjoy a wonderful trip just before the government started imposing restrictions. I was closely following the situation in Italy, which was the second worst affected country after China. Covid-19 was soon declared a pandemic, spreading globally at an alarming rate. Most of us Indians at that point were relaxed, thinking that summer was approaching in India. Since it seemed that the virus could multiply only in cold weather, it wouldn't be able to withstand the harsh Indian summer. We hoped that India would be spared. But this was wishful thinking and before we knew it, cases in India started rising exponentially with every day. Finally, on the 24th of March 2020, a complete lockdown was announced.

No shopping, no office, no movies in theatres and no hanging out with friends. Everything was closed. By then,

I hadn't even received a laptop from the office, so there was no question of work from home. It was as if destiny itself was trying to help us conceive by giving us a lot of quality time and relaxation together, which was very necessary. This was true for others as well, and as a result, the world saw a baby boom in the upcoming months of December and January.

During the initial lockdown phase of April, we had a rather good time at home. From sorting and re-arranging things in the cupboards to coffee dates in the balcony, we were doing all that we had done ages ago, given our hectic schedules. OTT, which is a household thing today, was just spreading its arms at that time. And it was an opportune time as people resorted to movies, web series and old TV shows to while away time. Government too started playing old TV shows like *Ramayana, Mahabharata* and many others to avoid people getting bored at home. Those who ventured out, without a valid purpose crowding the streets, usually returned home with a couple of long, red baton marks on their bums. It was sometimes funny to watch on television how police were beating those who were out without a reason. I used to be out only to buy veggies and groceries, and that too, just once a week.

In the first week of May, while watching the movie *Good News,* we were eagerly waiting for our own good news. We could relate to so many things while watching that movie. The 7th of May was approaching in a couple of days, when Deepika was supposed to take a home pregnancy test. We were very excited as well as desperate, hoping for the result to be positive.

Finally, that morning arrived. Ideally the urine pregnancy test is to be taken with the first sample of the morning. At 6 a.m., I was in a deep sleep, when Deepika shook me awake.

"Hey Sugu, I am pregnant! Yuppie!!" she announced dancing in joy, while I was yet to regain my senses.

Upon listening to what she said, I stood right up and hugged her. Such a joyful moment that was! I saw the test kit myself and hugged her again. We usually woke up late, but that morning was a new beginning. We paced up and down the balcony, planning on how to go ahead. We felt as though we had to plan it all immediately. I then took a moment to remind myself that she was now pregnant and should have breakfast and rest, and so we did.

During the time we were planning to become parents, I had already completed my search for a good gynaecologist. The home testing kit result is not always a hundred percent reliable. So without waiting for a moment, I called up the gynaecologist and sought an appointment for that morning itself. Dr. Aggarwal, our gynaecologist, is very experienced and highly recommended by many people. She greeted us really well and briefed us about our upcoming schedule. She asked us to get some blood tests done to confirm the news and called us the next day.

She confirmed the pregnancy after looking at the reports. As per medical calculations, whenever a lady comes to know she is pregnant, she is already four weeks pregnant. We were given an estimated date of delivery for the second week of

January. Once again, happiness was in the air while the doctor was explaining the initial dos and don'ts. She prescribed some tablets, mainly nutritional supplements to be taken for the entire duration of pregnancy. A sonography was prescribed after two weeks to make sure everything was okay.

After coming home, we were very eager to break the news to our respective families. They had been waiting for it for a long time. We wanted to do something special for them while breaking the news, but nothing was possible with the lockdown in place. Our family, that stays in Akola, wouldn't be able to come anytime soon, nor could we go. All we could do was to see their reactions through a video call. My mother, as usual, had eyes full of tears of happiness. Both sets of parents were elated as they were going to become grandparents.

A couple of days later, my laptop was finally ready and it was delivered home. It was the end of 'No Work' for me and I had to start working from home from the very next day. My restful days had come to an end, but I did not have any complaints as the relaxation had already served its purpose. It was time to adapt to the new normal of working from home with virtual meetings. Zoom emerged as a new and preferred medium for group video calling and meetings. Families and friends communicated through zoom calls as well, as it had been more than a month since the lockdown had come into force. A webinar, which was a lesser-known term earlier, was now a new normal for people to attend.

The first eight to ten days of pregnancy went really well, without any trouble. It was just a sit back and relax phase for her. She used to spend a lot of time surfing the net on ways to lead her pregnancy in the best way possible – what's good for the baby, what's bad for the baby, and so on. A lot of suggestions were pouring in from our families as well. There is something known as 'garbh sanskar' in India, which literally means good impressions on the fetus. It revolves around the belief, more recently being said true, that the baby starts inculcating good impressions right from the stage when it is formed and grows in the mother's womb. By now, Deepika had begun listening to garbh sanskar videos and webinars. We'd listen to those shlokas or verses daily, as she wanted me to be a part of it as well.

After a couple of weeks, as suggested by our gynaecologist, we went for our first sonography. The reports confirmed that the fetus was indeed in the uterus. The growth was normal and there was adequate amniotic fluid for the baby's growth. Until now, it was just our family who knew the good news apart from the two of us. None of our friends were aware of it yet. In most parts of India, a pregnancy is kept a secret within the family itself for the first three months. They believe that the first three months are crucial for the baby to gain strength and not get miscarried. Hence the news is broken only after completion of the first trimester.

Deepika and I, however, did not believe in this and were very eager to share our happiness with our friends as well. At least with our close ones.

We called Pratique first, as the memories of the northeast trip were still fresh. We were expecting that he'd be really excited. But as Deepika broke the news to him, he remained silent for a second, and then said "Okay..." as if he was waiting for her to finish and had something to say. Once she finished, he announced.

"Mayuri and I are expecting as well!"

Wow! That was an amazing bit of news and it was a huge return surprise. They were just a couple of weeks ahead of us. We didn't know about each other's plans of starting a family during the trip, so the pregnancies were a huge surprise. It was exciting that we'd be sharing this journey with our friends.

Everything was fine until week five or six. It was a heavenly feeling for Deepika to be pregnant till then. Very soon, as the doctor had told us to expect, she started feeling nauseated and would throw up very often. It was normal in the first trimester as the pregnancy hormones start growing rapidly in the body. The doctor advised her to keep eating every now and then, so that the energy levels didn't lower due to frequent vomits. Forget eating, even the smell of food would turn her nauseous. The honeymoon period of the first few days was over and now it was nowhere even close to the heavenly feeling of having a baby that we had experienced initially.

Soon, we faced a major challenge. I had to dedicate my day entirely to work, so I was not able to cook. Deepika's work from home had not yet started, but she couldn't cook at all because of her nausea that was triggered by the smell of food. The moment she entered the kitchen, she would get that feeling. Our parents couldn't come over any time soon as inter district travel was banned due to the Covid situation. Even maids were not allowed to work at that time. So, I decided to take some time out from work and meetings to cook our meals. There was no other option.

Though I am not a great cook, I knew the basics as I had cooked for myself for a few months when I was in the UK. It started off well, but gradually she started getting bored of the same old dishes as they didn't have a lot of variations. Even a normal person would tire of it, forget about a pregnant lady who has different cravings. Considering the situation, she somehow adjusted without complaints, but couldn't eat much, plus the series of throw ups. Unless something suited her taste buds, she wasn't able to swallow it. Not her fault, all thanks to the pregnancy hormones. She would often try some weird combinations like dal and rice with watermelon bites to force herself to eat. Items like khichdi, dal and rice, dosa, idly, and potato curry were repeated so much, that even today she shies away from them. Due to all this food mess, I began to get a bit concerned about whether she was getting adequate nutrition for herself and the baby.

Even though she was managing with the food somehow, there was another challenge of being available to be present beside her every time she threw up, as she often had dizziness immediately after. I had to hold her every time, even if she was sitting, to prevent her from fainting. To avoid the smell of food, she used to keep the bedroom door shut while I was in the kitchen. Because of being a slow cook, I used to carry my phone everywhere, even in the bathroom, for her to be able to call me whenever she felt nauseated while I was not around. A tablet was prescribed to suppress her nausea, but even that hadn't helped. We just went with the flow as we knew this was a normal phase and would stop automatically at some point.

Initially, we had visits to the gynaecologist every alternate week. During week six, Deepika noticed some spotting a couple of times. Knowing it could be a sign of miscarriage in some cases, we visited our gynaecologist without wasting any time. She said Deepika would need to take progesterone injections twice a week for a couple of weeks. Also, apart from the regular nutritional supplements, progesterone tablets were prescribed for a month. Progesterone is basically a pregnancy hormone. Boosting this hormone in the body helps the uterus to carry on with the pregnancy and can prevent a miscarriage.

Thankfully, the spotting stopped after the progesterone treatment, and we were much relieved. But by that time, she faced another problem – constipation. Constipation is also quite common in pregnancy and the intensity varies from person to person. Mostly the causes are pregnancy hormones and iron supplements. In Deepika's case, she was taking both iron supplements as well as progesterone booster injections. Hence the severity was huge. For a couple of days, she was severely constipated. Typically, she avoids medicines unless they are absolutely necessary and relies mostly on home remedies. She does it at normal times also, and more to it, this time she was pregnant. Hence, she was reluctant to take any medicine assuming it would harm the baby. But no home remedy was working and the constipation was getting worse. The doctor advised her to take a laxative, but she waited for a day hoping the home remedies would work. It was a mistake. She had to take a stronger dose of the same medicine the next day. It was extremely painful for her when she could finally relieve herself. It was so severe that she could not even sit properly for the next few days. She then decided that she wouldn't be so averse to taking medicines henceforth.

We had our hands so full dealing with all these issues that we had forgotten to share the news with a few of our friends. I then called up Bose and Amit, who had been my roommates in engineering college. They were happy for us. We had all met in Lucknow a year ago at Bose's wedding. Sayali, who was a common friend for all of us since college days, was unaware too. Pratique and I, along with both the pregnant ladies, made a group call to her to break the news. And we informed our friend Vishal in the same manner. We had group calls with most of the friends who are common to me and Pratique to share both the good news together.

It was now time for another sonography. This one was to make sure whether the baby's heart had started beating. We were eagerly looking forward to hearing the heartbeat of our baby for the first time. Thankfully, the place where we used to go for sonography allowed me to come in while following

Covid appropriate protocol. Many other places banned entry of companions citing Covid reasons. Our heartbeats started racing as the scan was about to start. And then suddenly that magical sound of the baby's heartbeat reached our ears, thanks to the sonography machine that amplifies the beats so that doctor can hear and assess. It was a moment to be cherished. Our baby's heart had started beating. It was a wonderful feeling.

In the ninth week, around the beginning of June, we received another bit of good news. No, this time it wasn't about any pregnancy. We were happy and relieved to learn that our parents would be able to come over as lockdown restrictions were eased a bit. Inter-district road travel was allowed with prior permission. Immediately my parents applied for a pass and booked a cab to travel from Akola to Pune, as rail service was still suspended. On the way, they picked up my mother-in-law from her hometown Jalgaon and the three finally arrived on 14th June. On that very afternoon, we came to know about Sushant Singh Rajput's suicide news on television. For a few minutes, we were stunned as he was our favourite actor. The arrival of our parents in the evening thankfully helped us to get over this news quickly. It was a joyful reunion after a long time.

Ever since we both thought about starting a family, we were keen on having the delivery in Pune itself and not at Deepika's maternal home, as is usually the custom, for two reasons. First and most important, we wanted to be together all along this journey. I did not want her to be without me by her side, hundreds of miles away, in case of an emergency situation.

Secondly, the quality of medical and emergency care facilities that we have in Pune were not available in her hometown. So, we requested our parents from both sides to stay with us and take care of her right here in Pune.

The arrival of our parents brought me the biggest relief. Relief from cooking! I got bored of it anyway. Even Deepika's mom joined my parents and came over so that her daughter gets to eat the food that she likes since childhood. Both the grannies-to-be started fulfilling the cravings of the mother-to-be happily. I was happy too, getting fed well along with Deepika. Finally, some variety in food after a long time. I was now able to be by Deepika's side for most of the time. I set up my workstation in the bedroom itself. It was a clear instruction from the parents that my duty was to be with her only and they would take care of every other thing at home. Work from home was helping a lot as I could take breaks as and when needed.

Apart from garbh sanskar for the baby, Deepika firmly believed in going through the stories of great people to learn from their lives. Chhatrapati Shivaji Maharaj was her role model. He was a great warrior. She found an old series on the life of Shivaji Maharaj and started watching it. I often joined her whenever I had the time.

After a couple of weeks, around week twelve, it was the time for a very important scan known as the NT scan. It checks whether there are any disorders or diseases in the baby that are hereditary. Once again, we were excited to see our baby. In the last scan while checking the heartbeat, the baby was visible just like a rounded yolk with few dots and a mass with cardiac activity. This time we were expecting the fetus to look more like a baby. And as expected we did see a baby. The head, neck, and body could be seen rather clearly. Though all the parts were not yet developed, it clearly resembled a baby. The more often we were seeing our baby growing inside, the more we were getting attached to him or her. And yes, the scan was all fine. Our baby was perfectly normal without any inherited deviations.

The following week was the end of Deepika's first trimester. Usually nausea and vomiting last until the first trimester, but in her case, they seemed to be nowhere on the verge of ending. She'd throw up at least once or twice a day. Food wise at least, since both her mother and mother-in-law were present, they were ensuring that she ate something or the other, and received her and the baby's quota of nutrition. Needless to say, Deepika, being a nutritionist herself, researched a lot about food. She read books and articles by some of the top nutritionists, Rujuta Diwekar being her favourite. She'd convey the recipes to our master-chef moms, who in turn would churn out the delicacies.

After a few weeks, I had one sleepless night. I continuously threw up for a whole night because of hyperacidity and acid reflux. For a moment, I wondered whether her pregnancy had transferred to me! Jokes apart, I had a history of hyperacidity. I used to have acidity issues since my college days, probably because I had to eat outside, and I was fond of spicy food. In 2018, I was diagnosed with abdominal tuberculosis and since then, my eating was limited and the doctor restricted my food to be almost zero spicy. The disease was treated and cured eventually, but I forgot that I was still advised to continue the same food habits. Ever since the supermoms arrived, they made sure I wasn't deprived of my favourite dishes that included a lot of chillies and spices. Ultimately, my stomach responded that night.

In the morning, I was dehydrated because of vomiting and became very weak with nausea. I was immediately hospitalised and given IV fluids which was the only way to recover from such an episode as I knew from my prior experience. I got the gastroscopy done and thankfully nothing serious was found, apart from some erosions in the stomach and esophagus which were cured over time. Deepika, in spite of being pregnant, got me hospitalised. Ultimately, Pratique arrived to stay with me, so I asked her to leave because she was more prone to catch an infection, as the hospital had some Covid patients as well. A couple of days later, I was discharged.

Around week sixteen, she completed watching all the episodes of the Shivaji Maharaj series. The garbh sanskar videos continued. Chandragupta Maurya was another personality whom she followed. She had already watched a series on his life, even before pregnancy. She was now looking for another historical personality to be inspired by. Shivaji Maharaj and Chandragupta Maurya were both great warriors and they taught one how to love and protect one's motherland. But this time, she wanted someone who believed in peace, someone who had full control over his mind and heart, someone who was calm, composed and a preacher of peace. The name that came into mind was none other than that of Gautam Buddha. He was the greatest proponent of peace in this world. Billions of people follow his teachings. So far, Deepika knew about him only as what was taught in history books. I suggested her to watch a series on the life of Gautam Buddha. I even got her a book, but she liked to watch rather than read. She found an old TV series on OTT and started watching it earnestly, while I joined her whenever time permitted. I requested her to tell me what happens in every episode after my work, so that even I would learn from his life without needing to watch it again by myself.

On the 1st of August, which is her birthday, we decided to do something special at home. It wasn't feasible to go out as Covid restrictions were still on. So far, we hadn't done any tree plantation activity together. So, along with our family, we planted a couple of saplings in the garden of our society. One of them was her all-time favourite parijaat or night blooming jasmine.

A couple of days later, Pratique and Mayuri arrived to celebrate two occasions. One was her birthday and the other was Raksha Bandhan. Since our initial days, Pratique and Deepika shared a brother-sister bond, and Pratique came home every year to celebrate the festival. It was a special celebration this time as Deepika and Mayuri were both pregnant and were meeting for the very first time after getting the good news. They were just days apart, and needless to say, both the moms-to-be exchanged much joy that day. It was a very special moment.

After carrying on for some time with the routine pregnancy life, week twenty arrived. It was the time for the most important scan. It's called an anomaly scan. By this time, all of the body parts of the baby are fully developed and from here on they just keep growing. This scan intends to check for any anomaly in the baby, meaning if the baby has all the body parts properly developed or if there is some abnormality. This time, for the scan, we went to the hospital that we had chosen for delivery, as it had modern-day machines for scanning. We went there one fine evening and to our surprise, I was not allowed to go even beyond the security desk due to strict Covid protocols. Only patients were allowed in. So far, I used to go in with her for all her scans by following Covid appropriate behaviour at our nearby radiologist. We used to watch the baby and listen to his or her heartbeat together during every scan. This time it seemed that she had to go in alone. She was not happy; nor was I. She went in without me quite reluctantly and I calmly waited downstairs as the scan usually takes an hour or sometimes even longer.

I don't know how, but she convinced the radiologist to allow me in at least for the last few minutes. I was very surprised when I was called by the security guard. He asked me to wear the safety gear and go in. The radiologist was very kind and chose not to dishearten Deepika as she was repeatedly requesting for me. She showed me how the baby was frequently moving inside, due to which it which took her a long time to finish the scan. The baby was doing fine without any abnormal anatomy as per the reports. We were very happy to know all was well. After close to three hours, we were finally back home.

It was almost the end of her second trimester and she was doing well. The nausea had finally stopped. She was now fine and was enjoying her time with the baby, who had by now started kicking. Everything was going good, as per the plan, and things were under control. We just hoped that all goes fine in the time to come and the third trimester would also be a smooth and comfortable ride.

3

THE UNINVITED DEVIL – CANCER

During all of her pregnancy so far, there was one thing making her uncomfortable, apart from the usual pain and discomfort that pregnancy entails. It was the cyst in her breast. A cyst is basically a lump or mass that can grow in any healthy organ or part of the human body. There are various causes that can form lumps inside the body and most of them are harmless. In Deepika's case, she had a bit of a history regarding this cyst.

While she was still in her second year of graduation, around six years ago, she felt a tiny lump in her left breast. She became a bit scared and had it checked by the doctor at her hometown. Some tests were performed at that time and it was found out that there was nothing to worry about. It was a fibroadenoma, meaning a solid firm lump of tissues which is benign or in simple words, not cancerous. She was relieved as the doctor said these usually occur in young women due to hormonal changes inside the body. There was no need to surgically remove the lump, as sometimes it gets dissolved on its own over time. Even if it didn't, it didn't cause any harm. Her lump didn't disappear, but over time, it did shrink. Sometimes it felt a bit bigger in size and sometimes very tiny. But it didn't hurt at all. Maybe its size used to vary in relation to her menstruation cycle. She decided not to pay attention to it anymore and continue her life as usual. Even after our wedding, we had got a mammogram done again in Pune, just to be doubly sure. It confirmed the lump as a fibroadenoma, so we became free of worry about the lump thereafter.

Coming back to her pregnancy, the same lump had started growing in size from around week six. Initially it did not raise any alarm as it used to grow and shrink in the past as well. But this time, it was not shrinking, but growing bigger week by week. She could feel it getting bigger and bigger. She was still okay with it, as we knew it was a fibroadenoma. During our visits to the gynaecologist, we always used to discuss this with her. She also told us that in pregnancy, usually such lumps occur in many women, and if some are already present, they grow. This is due to the rapid changes in the breasts as they get ready to perform their function of feeding the baby after birth.

Everyone whom we used to ask to said that these lumps are common in pregnancy and they go away on their own. We were relaxed about it, but just wanted that it shouldn't cause any pain. By week ten, the lump had rapidly grown to almost the size of a lemon. Then it started hurting her. My mom, well versed in Ayurvedic therapy, applied a special type of mud at the site to get relief from the pain, but it did not yield any relief. We thought of going in for homeopathic treatment and consulted our gynaecologist. She gave us a go ahead, to give it a try. We tried homeopathic medicine for a couple of weeks, but it was a failure too. The lump was getting bigger and bigger. Finally, our gynaecologist advised us to undergo a breast sonography as mammograms are generally not advised in pregnancy.

At around week thirteen, we got a breast sonography done. The radiologist performing sonography was a bit unsure about the diagnosis of the lump, which by now had grown to the size of a small pear. She took stock of the history from us, looked at all the previous reports and termed the lump as a giant fibroadenoma. The report showed the lump to be oval shaped, with the length being more than four centimetres and width just about two centimetres. We went back to our gynaecologist with the report. She suggested we leave the lump as it was for the time being, as it would anyway shrink and go away automatically once she delivers and finishes the lactation. In case it caused unbearable pain, she said that she would refer us to a breast specialist to look for surgical options to remove the lump. But that would be the worst-case scenario. At that point, our gynaec wanted surgery to be the last option as it would attract other mandates like anaesthesia, painkillers, and antacids, etc., which are big no-no during pregnancy.

The lump, however, was in no mood to stay at rest. It kept on increasing in size. The associated pain in the breast was intermittent, but it was getting sharper day by day. Deepika tried her best to ignore and not to get bothered with the lump for the next four to five weeks, but at one point she became frustrated, as she was not able to focus on the baby and her pregnancy because of the pain. Sometimes she couldn't even sleep properly. We then started to think in the direction of surgical options. Although no one likes to have surgery, but at one point you get tired of the pain and want the source of it to be out of your body as soon as possible. Also, a second thought was that the lump might further grow during lactation and it would not allow her to feed the baby. Hence, we got inclined towards getting it removed once and for all. The lump story so far was going on in parallel with the pregnancy, till the end of the previous chapter.

Around week twenty-two, which was the first week of September, a couple of weeks after the anomaly scan, we finally decided to go to the breast specialist to get rid of the lump. Dr. Pranjali, a renowned breast specialist and surgeon, whom we were supposed to meet, was known to our gynaecologist Dr. Aggarwal. She, while evaluating breast sonography report earlier, asked us to meet her if the pain got unbearable. So one fine Monday, we went to the hospital for consultation. She thoroughly examined Deepika and asked us for all the previous history associated with the lump. She also checked out the breast sonography report that we had done a couple of months ago.

Already frustrated with the lump, we were expecting a surgery to get it removed as soon as possible. However, Dr. Pranjali calmly rejected the option of surgery right then. She said that although such lumps usually occur or grow during pregnancy, unless we came to know the exact cause of it growing so rapidly, we couldn't go in for a surgery. She called us for a core needle biopsy to assess the nature of the lump. We were still pitching for fibroadenoma as the previous report showed the same. But she wanted to do a proper biopsy which had never been done in the past. In a core needle biopsy procedure, the lump site is numbed and a wide hollow needle is inserted to the core of the lump with the help of sonography. The needle takes out some mass containing tissues from inside the lump. Those tissues are then microscopically examined to see the nature of the cells within. That tells us what causes the lump to grow so rapidly. A couple of days later, on Wednesday, the core needle biopsy procedure was performed by the doctor. The removed mass was sent to pathology for examination and we were told that the report would be out in about three to four days.

We had no option, but to wait for a few more days. Meanwhile, I was neck-deep in work that week. I used to have meetings every now and then. My project had very tight deadlines and hence I was stuck to my laptop all the time. During work hours, I had to somehow manage those visits to the hospital. Deepika, in the meantime, had completed almost half of the Gautam Buddha series. Mostly, she used to play it with speakers on, so that I could listen in the background as I worked. I still remember the tune of the flute that Siddharth, as a prince, used to play in the episodes during that hectic week.

Four days after the biopsy procedure, the next Monday morning I received a call from the hospital. I went out of the room for attending this call as Deepika was watching her series with speakers on. I thought the reports were out and Dr. Pranjali would plan a surgery soon. But instead, the pathology staff told me that they would be doing some more tests on the same sample, and asked me to make an online payment for them. The amount was close to fifteen thousand rupees. They told me the names of the tests as ER, PR and HER2 markers. Initially, I thought they were suggesting some unnecessary tests. But then, as usual when I googled the names, I was stunned. For a few minutes, I started shivering. Those tests were meant for checking the type of cancer. For me, it was the shock of my life! Even while I am writing this, I am shivering. Let me get some fresh air before I can resume my narration.

Okay, so then after calming myself down as much as I could, I called up Dr. Pranjali immediately, and told her what the pathology lab wanted. She said yes, it was her who had instructed them to conduct those tests. She told me that the lump didn't seem to be a fibroadenoma. She confirmed that those marker tests were indeed related to cancer. The sample potentially resembled cancer, but they needed those tests to confirm the same. I told her that I was feeling a bit worried now. She, while calmly consoling me, said that I shouldn't panic and whatever it turned out to be, they had enough experience to handle it and would deal with it. I somehow managed to calm myself, called the hospital and paid the amount online.

The reports would be out in two to three days. I had to wait, steeped in worry till then.

It was a different me who went back to the bedroom after those calls.

"Is something wrong? You look upset," Deepika asked me while turning the speakers off as I sat down on my chair.

"No, just work stuff," I lied, trying to avoid eye contact.

For the first time, I was pretending to work, but my mind was completely occupied with the 'C' word. She was quietly watching the Buddha episode with a smile on her face. The more I was looking at her, the deeper I was falling into the well of stress. Needless to say, I had to hide it from her till the final reports were out and the diagnosis was confirmed. I couldn't tell my parents either, as they weren't strong enough to handle the news. Deepika, I knew, was strong enough, but she was almost six months pregnant by then, and I didn't want her to assume anything and worry till we had a confirmed diagnosis.

So it was me alone, who was dealing with this anxiety. Now every hour, every minute was a challenge for me to behave as though everything was normal. My mind was processing endless thoughts during the waiting period. We already had a tiny happy family on the cards, and now that one call had shattered all my happiness. Mom used to ask me why I was not eating well, and I just gave her silly excuses. Work wise, I had a tough time as well. During meetings, I was not able to speak much, as I used to be immersed in other thoughts. Somehow I managed my daily tasks, but they were not up to the mark. I was supposed to focus as the project had tight deadlines, but my subject of focus was just the 'C' word during that entire week.

Three days later, on Thursday I got a call from the hospital. It was the head pathologist herself this time. I asked her about the result of the tests. She said all three markers were negative. My second question was as quick as light,

"Then is it not cancer?"

She just conservatively said, "Your doctor will tell you that."

She had called me for the anomaly scan report, which I sent over to her right then. She said they were still doing some tests in-house and the results would be out the next day. To some extent, I felt relieved. I didn't have much knowledge about cancer until then. My naive logic was that since the marker tests were negative, there was no cancer.

The relief was the calm before the storm. The next day, reports were ready and we were called by the hospital to consult Dr. Pranjali. We were supposed to collect the reports from pathology lab and then go to her. While collecting the reports from the counter, I was so desperate to have a look at them, that I didn't even have the patience to show them to the doctor first. The most anxious moment that I had so far was the last ball of the 2007 T20 World Cup final between India and Pakistan. The anxiety levels, while I was taking out the reports from the envelope, were even worse than that last ball moment. I was just looking if the summary had some words like carcinoma, malignancy, etc., which all mean cancer. And my worst fear came alive. The result was the opposite to that of the final match.

The summary said that it was Invasive Ductal carcinoma, which is a type of breast cancer.

I was numb with shock all over again!

While we were waiting outside Dr. Pranjali's cabin, Deepika saw my upset face. I knew that she was much better and more composed than me while dealing with anxious situations, hence this time I gave her a hint that it could be cancer. She took it on a much lighter note and said, "Don't worry! Whatever it is, we will deal with it!"

That certainly gave me some courage to go into the doctor's cabin where the official confirmation was waiting for us.

Finally, we went inside. Dr. Pranjali just skimmed through the reports. She already knew the results as she was in continuous touch with the pathologist. She calmly conveyed to us that Deepika's lump was a pregnancy associated breast cancer. It's a rare disease and happens among one in three thousand pregnant women. The growth of the lump, or rather we can call it a tumour now, is fuelled by pregnancy hormones and hence it is known as pregnancy associated breast cancer. It can happen during the pregnancy or lactation period of one year after the pregnancy. My earlier assumption that negative markers meant no cancer, was wrong. It was actually a triple negative type of breast cancer.

As the doctor confirmed it was a cancer, the first thing I did was to look at Deepika's face. I was concerned about the stressful situation that was forced upon her at that moment, hence I checked whether she was ok to digest this news. She looked calm, but was more concerned about what would happen to the baby. Once Dr. Pranjali saw that the news had sunk in, she started telling us what to do next.

The priority of the treatment would aim to get Deepika free of cancer first, and the next priority would be to save the baby. At some point during treatment, she would need surgery to remove the tumour, but the question was when to do the surgery. The first line of treatment in breast cancer is surgery; but in her case, as she was six months pregnant, surgery didn't seem to be a feasible option at that point. It would need her to be in general anaesthesia for a very long time. In addition, the painkillers and other drugs post-surgery were not advisable for the mother and baby. Hence the doctor advised us to go for chemotherapy first, which would shrink the tumour till she delivered. Once the baby was out, they would surgically remove the residual tumour.

Obviously, we had a lot of questions and the doctor did not hesitate to answer all of them patiently. The very first one was what would happen to the baby. The doctor said that usually it is safe to have chemotherapy in the third trimester, but there was a risk that the baby might be delivered prematurely. Abortion was not an option at that time as the pregnancy was already in its twenty fourth week. We had to go ahead with the risk as we did not have any other option. We could not delay the treatment further or else the cancer could grow beyond control.

Dr. Pranjali being a surgeon herself, explained to us that there were two types of surgeries – one known as mastectomy in which the entire breast would be removed, and the other was lumpectomy where only the lump or the tumour area would be removed while the rest of the breast would be conserved. This type of surgery was also known as breast conservation surgery. Whatever we go with, it was supposed to happen only after the delivery. The doctor told us that this would be a multidisciplinary treatment and we would go step by step towards our target of getting Deepika cancer-free. The first step was chemotherapy, so that once the tumour started shrinking in size, the pain she was going through, because of the size of the tumour, would also gradually subside. She referred us to Medical Oncologist Dr. Tushar who would first take over the treatment for chemotherapy. He would tell us in detail the effects and risk factors of chemotherapy in her case. We were supposed to meet him the next day.

The meeting inside Dr. Pranjali's cabin was life changing. I was thankful that after coming out, Deepika was still composed. The word 'cancer', which so far had just been heard and read about, was now being felt by her.

"I have always been a fitness enthusiast and have followed a healthy lifestyle. Why did I get cancer?" Deepika questioned as we headed back home.

I was even more upset, but I consoled her, “We will get over this, trust me. Everything will turn out fine in the end.”

It wasn’t her mistake; she was just that one unlucky pregnant woman among three thousand others.

The next task was to inform the family, they didn’t even have a hint of the C word yet. They were just concerned about the lump giving her pain and wanted it to be removed as soon as it was possible. I gathered the courage and gently informed our parents about the diagnosis. They were shocked and nervous as expected, and began to worry about what would happen next. Taking a lead, Deepika made them understand that it was what it was. All we could do was to face it. I wondered how she was still so cool, even though she had got to know that she had cancer only an hour ago. She even requested mom to prepare something sweet to eat and to celebrate. Mom could not understand what she was up to. She, anyway, filled a couple of bowls with kheer and served us. Deepika, not sure from where she gathered such a brave heart, said,

“The worst that could happen has happened. Now let’s face it with a sweet beginning.”

I, however, was not so cool. The anxiety that I was going through for a week was now gone, but it left me with a host of reasons to worry.

What would happen?

Would the chemotherapy work?

Would the baby tolerate it?

And most importantly, would Deepika come out of the treatment safely?

My mind was flooded with questions I had no answers to.

Looking at the way Deepika accepted the fact in such a sporting spirit, I spoke my heart out to her that evening. For the first time after so many years, my eyes were full of tears while I was describing my ordeal of the last few days. She understood why I had been upset the past week. She consoled me saying that she had accepted it. She had a baby inside and she would undergo the treatment positively and patiently for the sake of the baby. I was amazed by her positivity.

To some extent, I was also heading towards accepting the reality. While going to bed that night, I was just thinking about the next day's meeting with Dr. Tushar. I called up Pratique immediately and gave him the news. He judged from my voice that I was tensed. He offered to come to our place right away, but I told him that I didn't have the stamina to stay awake any longer. I asked him to come along with us to visit the doctor the next day. He was the only close friend who was staying in Pune at that time and I wanted him to be by our side while we would be making some crucial decisions. I still don't remember how many times I suddenly woke up that night with thoughts running amok in my head.

The next day Pratique joined us when we went back to the hospital to meet Dr. Tushar for chemotherapy related planning. Dr. Pranjali had already briefed him about Deepika. It was a much better day as anxiety of the result was over and we freely discussed the future course of treatment with the doctor. He examined her and started explaining to us about the condition and treatment. The first line of treatment for her was chemotherapy. The plan was to have twelve sessions of chemo, starting as soon as possible. They would be administered once a week in a daycare facility. It was her twenty fourth week and the target was to finish all twelve before the baby was delivered. Considering forty weeks of pregnancy, we had additional three to four weeks in hand as a buffer if she couldn't tolerate it and wanted to have breaks in between the chemo sessions. Followed by these twelve sessions of chemo, delivery would take place. And after the delivery, she would have a surgery to remove the residual cancerous tumour. Once she recovered from surgery, again she would have to undergo four chemo sessions of different medicines. After that, radiation therapy was the final line of treatment. All this was supposed to last for the next nine to ten months.

Now, all this sounded like a plan, but there was one big risk as we had been briefed by Dr. Pranjali. Dr. Tushar confirmed the same – the effect of chemo medicine could trigger labour pain earlier than expected. He said we would have to make up our minds for a premature baby, just in case. Also, there was a risk of intrauterine growth retardation, termed usually as IUGR. It means that even if the baby is not born preterm, there was a chance that the growth of the baby while inside the mother, might get hampered due to the chemo. But as I said earlier, we did not have a choice.

The next thing that the doctor conveyed hurt Deepika even more than the news of the cancer itself. It was hard to digest the fact that she wouldn't be able to feed the baby once he or she was born. She would be finishing twelve chemo sessions by the time the baby was born, and even after the delivery, she would be continuing with the remaining chemo cycles. Hence the doctor strictly said no to mother's milk as the toxic chemo medicine may pass on to the infant. I didn't feel it was a major problem, but for a mother, not allowing her to feed her baby is something equivalent to not allowing her to breathe. Breastfeeding not only provides food to the baby, but facilitates the growth of a mother's special bond with the baby. This was the only thing I saw that made her really upset during this entire episode. The whole point of going to the doctor earlier, to get rid of the lump, was to be able to breastfeed without any pain. And after everything, breastfeeding itself was off the charts. This was emotionally painful, really painful.

After coming back home, to cheer her up, I convinced her that she need not worry. Later, who knows, she may be able to feed the baby after all. Maybe we could delay the surgery after birth or maybe we could delay the chemo, but we would ensure that she fed the baby somehow. I knew from inside that this would not be possible, but I still made her a false promise to lessen her pain. It was very important that she went ahead with a happy and positive attitude rather than a sorrowful one, and hence I let her be in that assurance. I decided not to discuss anything about breastfeeding with the doctor until the baby was born.

Before going ahead with the first session of chemotherapy, the doctor prescribed some tests to rule out metastasis, which is the spread of cancer to other parts of the body. For this, a full body PET scan is the test that is usually done. But in Deepika's case it was not an option as the test cannot be done on a pregnant woman. Hence, both the doctors decided to safely scan individual parts where it was most likely to spread. Sonography of the abdomen and pelvis, 2D echo for the heart and a chest X-ray were prescribed. Even an X-ray is not safe during pregnancy, but it was carefully done using an abdominal shield. Thankfully, all other examined areas were okay without any abnormal growths, lumps or metastasis.

The previous day had been Friday, a working day, and I forgot that after receiving a call from the hospital, we had rushed to collect reports and meet the doctor immediately. In all of this, I had left my laptop as it was, and had disappeared without letting anybody know. After finishing those tests, I realised that I needed to inform my office as they knew nothing about what was going on. I immediately switched it on, plugging in the charger as the battery was drained by now. There were countless mails and chat messages for me, right from senior managers to my peers as there was a milestone deadline the previous day and I had disappeared all of a sudden. There were so many missed calls that I noticed later. I sent a mail to my manager with everyone in the loop and informed them all that had been happening. Thankfully no one asked me about work in their replies and were only concerned about Deepika's health.

In order to plan the chemotherapy sessions and have a final discussion with Dr. Tushar, I called up my sister Pranali, who happens to be a doctor as well. She was practicing as a general physician in Nagpur at that time. She immediately came down to Pune after learning about her sister-in-law's health. She told us that she would be with us until the treatment started and was streamlined. It was reassuring that we had a doctor at home, so that she could speak to the treating doctors in medical terms. She also assessed the test reports so far and agreed with what the doctors were planning for Deepika.

Before going ahead with the chemotherapy, I was looking for a second opinion on the diagnosis of breast cancer. Vishal, who too stays in Nagpur, had many contacts with experts in the field of cancer as his father had also suffered from cancer a few years ago. Through one of his friends, I got the reference and contact details of a senior pathologist Dr. Roshan Chinoy, who had more than three decades of experience in diagnostic pathology at the Tata Memorial Hospital, Mumbai. She was at that time the head of the pathology department at a renowned hospital in Mumbai. She was extremely kind when I spoke to her and she agreed to test Deepika's sample herself.

We had to act quickly as we couldn't afford to delay the chemo. Pratique immediately offered to drive me to Mumbai and deliver the samples to Dr. Chinoy personally. We collected them from our Pune hospital on Monday morning and left for Mumbai to be back on the same day. As usual, he was the only driver, driving to and from Mumbai. I was rather shameless to let him drive all these years on all our road trips, not having learnt to drive myself. Anyway, we delivered the samples at her hospital, but the result would not be out for a couple of days at least, as they had to prepare slides from the blocks first and then assess the slides. On Wednesday morning, I received the report through email. Somewhere in my heart, I was hoping that the earlier reports would be proved wrong. Unfortunately, they weren't. At least now we didn't have any repentance for not having done a double check on such a major diagnosis.

On the same day, we were supposed to meet Dr. Tushar with the latest reports as well as the reports of the second opinion. This time we were joined by both Pratique and Pranali during the discussion. Dr. Chinoy was kind enough to speak to Dr. Tushar personally, and shared her observations on Deepika's samples. Accordingly, he finalised the treatment plan. He even spoke to Dr. Aggarwal, our gynaecologist, who had not been in the picture for the past couple of weeks while we were getting the lump checked by Dr. Pranjali. He conveyed the situation to her and sought her go-ahead from the pregnancy point of view. Starting the next day, Deepika was supposed to take her first chemo session. The doctor also told us that Deepika would lose all her hair after a couple of chemo sessions. She would have to live with no hair till she completed all her chemo cycles. He said that they'd grow back once we were done with all the chemo sessions. On a lighter note, he even said that he'd give us a full refund if the hair didn't grow back.

After the consultation, we went for a quick visit to the daycare facility at the hospital. That place was going to be her home once a week for the next twelve weeks. Dr. Tushar gave us a rough estimation of the entire treatment charges. Although we had medical insurance, the overall costs were going to be much above its coverage. But we had no other option, so we made up our mind to use our savings to support the remaining cost of treatment Finally, the diagnosis part was over and now the main battle was about to begin from the next day – the fight with cancer.

4

THE ONSET OF CHEMOTHERAPY

Thursday, 24th September, 2020

It was the day that the doctors would start giving Deepika medicines that no expectant mother would ever wish to get injected into her body. Many people advise a pregnant woman to not take even a simple cold and cough tablet. And here was Deepika, about to have chemotherapy, the whole purpose of which was to kill the growing cells inside the body. The doctors had already told us that there was a risk of growth retardation of the baby or premature delivery, but we had to go ahead with it, as her life was at risk if we didn't.

We reached the hospital in the morning at eight. Pranali had accompanied us. This time I took a day's leave from the office in advance, as it was supposed to be a full-day procedure. Dr. Tushar had asked us to meet Dr. Jyoti, who was in-charge at Daycare. He would visit in the afternoon, but he had already passed on the details of chemotherapy medicines or regimen, as they commonly call it, which Deepika was supposed to be administered. Upon entry, the nurse asked us to take bed no 1, which was right in front of the nursing counter. Deepika didn't seem very comfortable with it, as it was near the entry door and close to everybody passing by. I asked the nurse to give us another bed, but she was a bit reluctant. I heard someone calling Deepika from behind the counter. It was Dr. Jyoti, head of the daycare staff. I immediately went to her. She said that Dr. Tushar had instructed them to keep Deepika right in front of their eyes at all times for monitoring. It was a rare case of a pregnant patient undergoing chemotherapy, hence they did not want to take any chances.

Dr. Jyoti was very kind and soft spoken from the beginning. She arranged another bed for Deepika, which was further away from the entry gate. Deepika was comfortable with it this time. A nurse was, however, instructed to pass by her every now and then, and monitor her. Deepika parked herself on the bed, waiting for further instructions. In the meantime, Dr. Jyoti gave me an admission note which I was supposed to go out and show at the admission counter to register Deepika as admitted. Once done with that, the doctor ordered her medicine from the pharmacy which was located just downstairs.

While Deepika was waiting for the medicines, I was called by Dr. Jyoti at the nursing counter. She asked me to sign a couple of undertaking forms similar to what a relative of a patient signs before any surgery. Every form was printed, except one. The risks associated with chemotherapy were mentioned on the undertaking forms for usual patients. Since Deepika's case was rare, they did not have any standard printed form stating risks for pregnant women. So, that one form was handwritten by Dr. Jyoti herself. As briefed by Dr. Tushar a day before, it mentioned the risks associated with the baby. It stated for me that,

'I am aware that the growth of the fetus could be hampered due to chemotherapy and it can even be born prematurely. I understand this and still give my consent to go ahead with the procedure'.

Although not happy to accept, I did not hesitate to sign as we had already discussed this umpteen times since the cancer was diagnosed. Deepika too was aware of this and we had made up our minds. Without giving a second thought, I signed it and gave the team my go-ahead to proceed with the chemo.

Finally, her medicines were ready. A couple of nurses came in and asked me and Pranali to wait outside. They were about to insert an intracath into her vein, to deliver the medicines. Chemotherapy medicines are generally administered to the patient after dilution in a bottle of IV fluid, or 'saline' in layman's language. The solution has to be given at the fixed rate of flow, hence they brought in an infusion pump for her. It's a device through which the pipe of the IV fluid passes, which controls the flow rate or speed of the fluid delivered to the patient. They inserted an intracath in a vein behind her right palm and started administering the medicines through it. Initially they injected pre-medicines for some time. Pre medicines included antacids, anti-allergic medicines, mild pain relievers, etc., in order to keep the side effects of actual chemo medicines minimal. Also, a digital monitor, BP cuff and an oximeter were connected to monitor her condition. An oxygen supply mask was also ready by her side, in case needed.

After a couple of hours, the nurse finally connected the first bottle of chemo medicine. As usual, my inner Google woke up and I checked the label of the medicine. It was named Paclitaxel. I am sure no one reading this would be interested in knowing the names of medicines, but please bear with my silly hobbies. This medicine would take three hours to be administered. Accordingly, the nurse set the timing on the infusion pump and she started the flow. Deepika was ready, prepared to be patient and bear whatever discomfort followed. Initially she felt it was like usual saline, but as time passed, she started feeling a bit light headed. She just sat back and relaxed with closed eyes. Something was going on in her mind, but I didn't realise it at that time.

After a couple of hours, all three of us had our lunch, which we had brought from home. I thought they would pause the medicine till she had food, but the IV was running in one hand, and with the other hand she had her meal. Dr. Tushar visited in the afternoon and checked whether everything was going as per plan. He enquired if she had some discomfort. Dr. Jyoti also dropped in every thirty minutes and asked Deepika how she was feeling. They had an entire emergency line up ready in case of any potential reaction of the medicine. Dr. Jyoti was heard telling the nurse that she would not pardon even a small mistake in monitoring her condition.

Once the Paclitaxel IV was over, they connected another chemo medicine known as Carboplatin. This was supposed to go on for another hour. She took a nap while this medicine was going in. This was followed by a small plain IV without medicine, or flush as they call it, that was to last for about thirty minutes. While the flush was going on, Dr. Jyoti visited us again and asked Deepika how the experience of her first chemo had been. Overall, she had tolerated the chemo well and she was apparently doing fine without any complications. The doctor was very happy with her positive attitude. In a casual chat after the medicines were over, she took stock of her pregnancy story so far and asked us not to worry and keep up with the same spirit. The first chemo was finally over and we headed back home.

While in the cab en route home, I asked Deepika, "What were you thinking with your eyes closed as you lay on the bed during chemo? In spite of feeling light headed, you looked so calm."

Her reply was unimaginable. She smiled as she told me the same.

"Do you remember I had watched a series on Chandragupta Maurya during the first trimester? Chanakya was Chandragupta's guru. They were an ideal pair of guru-shishya, or teacher-disciple. The intelligence of Chanakya is well known in the history of mankind. Once, a cruel king Dhananand separated Chanakya from Chandragupta and lodged him in jail. He wanted Chanakya to forget everything and destroy his intelligence. He used to inject him with a little poison daily to erase his memory, but Chanakya was not the one to be vanquished. While he would feel drowsy every time the poison was injected, he'd relax, close his eyes and chant continuously that 'his name is Chanakya and Chandragupta is his disciple'. He'd chant this single sentence hundreds of times until he fully regained his senses. He wanted to remember only this one thing. He was sure that one day, Chandragupta would definitely free him and take him away from Dhananand. Till that time, he just wanted to remember his name, as he knew that Chandragupta would bring back the rest of his memory."

Deepika continued that, while there was no exact correlation between Chanakya's story and hers, she correlated her chemo with the poison. While it was being injected, she just kept herself relaxed. With her eyes closed, she thought continuously,

"I have a baby inside me and I have to live, be happy and keep myself well to look after him or her."

This was the only thing she thought about throughout the procedure. Ultimately the medicine finished and she felt better. After her response, I kept looking at her with a smile. My heart was full of pride. I was amazed at her grit, even when the odds were against her. I was lucky to call her mine. I now realised why she used to watch the series on great personalities with such devotion. Not only did she watch them, but she also applied their life events, their principles in her own life.

Overall, the administration of the first chemo went off well. Now it was the time to be ready for its side effects. The immediate effect that made all of us worry was that there was a significant reduction in the baby's movements after the chemo that evening. Before the chemo, the baby had started kicking and Deepika would feel the baby's movements throughout the day. Even during the scans, the radiologist used to show us how the baby was moving inside her. But that day, ever since the chemo medicine was injected, there was hardly any movement of the baby. Even during the night, when the baby used to be most active, it wasn't kicking. We were worried a bit, but just went ahead with the medications and routine, hoping that she'd get to feel the movements soon, but it didn't happen that night. However, the next morning, she again felt the kicks and we breathed a big sigh of relief.

While the baby's movement started again, the body pain associated with chemo also began. The feeling of light-headedness, nausea and tiredness persisted the entire day. The doctor had already prescribed some medicines in advance to cope up with these side effects, but they did not help beyond some extent. Since she was pregnant, she did not want to take a pile of painkillers every now and then as the side effects were now expected to be persistent till all of the chemo cycles were over. Another side effect of chemo medicine was constipation. She had severe constipation the next day, as the prescribed dose of laxatives wasn't enough. I immediately called up Dr. Jyoti and got it increased. After a couple of days, the issue was resolved.

The medicines of chemotherapy typically retard the production of white blood cells or WBCs in our body, which highly increase the chances of infection in a person undergoing treatment. To get over this, an injection of a medicine known as Filgrastim was prescribed to Deepika, to be taken two days after each chemo. This injection boosts WBC production inside the body. Hence on Saturday evening, Pranali gave her the injection. It was supposed to be taken subcutaneously, meaning below the skin surface at the areas like stomach or thigh where there are a lot of fat tissues. She preferred to get it injected in her thigh.

The next day onwards, Deepika began suffering from immense pain in her back and joints. So much so that we had to call Dr. Jyoti and ask her for a remedy. The overall pain due to this injection was even worse than the chemo medicine itself. She even developed a fever. A higher dose of paracetamol was prescribed to reduce the pain. As there were limitations on the pain relief medication she was allowed, paracetamol was the best bet that we could go for. She was supposed to bear with anything beyond that.

Next day, Dr. Pranjali called me to enquire about Deepika's health. I raised the point regarding the filgrastim injection. She explained the mechanism of that medicine. Basically WBCs are created in our bone marrow. Filgrastim stimulates, rather pokes our bone marrow to make more WBCs. That way, the required number of WBCs are maintained and a person is protected from infection. Since the bones are forced to work more, they resist and cause pain, especially in the joints. But this medicine was a must have after every chemo. She had to be free from any infection throughout the treatment, otherwise it would be a much bigger thing to deal with. Due to this, we had to also ensure thorough cleanliness and sanitation at home at all times.

Deepika's brother Jayesh and her sister-in-law Kajal arrived from Mumbai as soon as they came to know about the cancer. They wanted to be with her during these difficult times. Deepika shared a very friendly bond with her brother and he too kept entertaining her and all of us, as he was a pro in acting and mimicry. He kept our spirits up. One fine evening, a couple of days after this injection, we all were sitting in our bedroom and having a casual conversation when Deepika suddenly broke down. She was trying to divert her attention from the pain by chatting on random subjects, but at one point, it became unbearable. This was the fourth day after chemo, a day when the pain was at its peak. She managed to resume the conversation with a smile, thanks to our mimicry artist who was trying his best to make his sister forget the pain.

Meanwhile, all of us were planning to do a maternity photoshoot the next day. I know it was too early as it is usually done in the ninth month, and it was just her seventh. But in our case, as Dr. Tushar said, Deepika would lose her hair after a couple of chemo sessions. We had limited time. One was already over, so she insisted on getting the photoshoot done before the second. Jayesh, Kajal and Pranali started painting posters and placards for the photoshoot, while Pratique and Mayuri arranged maternity gowns and other props for her.

The fifth day after the chemo was much better compared to the past four days of pain and side effects. Finally, we could focus on the baby and speak to him or her as we usually used to do before the cancer. One of the points of garbh sanskar was that both mother and father should keep talking to the baby. This way, both the voices become familiar to the baby, and it becomes easier for him or her to recognise them once he or she is born. After spending some quality time together in the morning, we got ready for the photoshoot. Deepika looked very happy donning a pretty maternity gown. For a few hours, we just forgot about the cancer and enjoyed our shoot wholeheartedly. Pranali left for Nagpur the very same evening as she had to return to work the next day.

On day six, Deepika was supposed to undergo some blood tests to check whether all her blood parameters were okay and whether any adverse effect of the chemo had taken place that could delay the next session. Thankfully, all was good, and WBC level was also maintained. Dr. Tushar gave us the go ahead for the next chemo, which was scheduled after a couple of days. This was supposed to be a repetitive cycle now, for the next eleven weeks. Day one chemo, day three filgrastim injection, day six blood tests and day eight, again the next chemo. In a week, she was expected to bear three needle pricks. One for inserting the intracath, one for the injection and one for the blood sample extraction. I was amazed at how she was still so calm and composed, and bearing all the pain stoically. It was a long battle ahead, but I was convinced by now that she had all the qualities of a warrior.

5

INJECTION

On Thursday, 1st October 2020, we went to the hospital again for the second session of chemo. This time, it was just Deepika and I. Jayesh, Kajal and Pranali had returned home after lending their support during the tough start. The same bed was allocated to her, and the nurses came in to start the medications again. This time, the intracath was inserted into the left arm as there was still some swelling in the right arm due to the previous week's intracath. First pre-medications, followed by both the chemo IVs and finally flush IV. Medicines, procedure, duration, everything was the same as the first session. This time too she closed her eyes and relaxed, meditating as the session continued.

While the last medicine was being administered, Dr. Jyoti told me that we had to additionally administer an IV containing an iron injection. Her haemoglobin was found to be on the lower side in the latest blood reports and it could go further down due to the chemo, which would not be good for her and the baby. Iron increases the haemoglobin and hence they decided to give her an iron injection after taking our gynaecologist Dr. Aggarwal into confidence. A small test shot of iron has to be given to the patient first, to check if he or she develops any reaction. Only then the full injection could be given. A nurse came in and administered her a test shot on her forearm opposite to the one where the IV was attached. It was a sharp and painful shot. Her right arm was burning like fire for some time. But there wasn't any blistery skin reaction or rash. Hence, they went ahead with giving her the iron IV. Although there wasn't any rash due to the shot, a large dark mark was formed on her arm which is as it is even today. I am not sure whether the nurse had made some mistake while giving the shot. We anyway didn't pay heed to it at that time as the other things we were dealing with were much bigger than the mark.

This time as we reached home, Deepika experienced shortness of breath and a lot of fatigue while climbing up the stairs. Our home is on the first floor and unfortunately the building does not have an elevator. Hence, she had no option but to climb a couple of dozen stairs. Weight gain due to the baby and the chemo effect on the body were aggravating factors for her fatigue. Once we were inside, I pulled out a chair to let her sit right next to the door till she regained her normal breathing. This wasn't anticipated. While I was expecting it towards the end of her pregnancy, this had come a bit too early. The chemo sessions were lowering her stamina at a fast rate.

Like the previous time, she was supposed to take side-effects minimising medications aggressively for the next two to three days. A higher dose of laxative was prescribed this time to keep constipation at bay. A couple of days later, we went to the hospital for the filgrastim injection, as this time Pranali was not available to administer it to her. I remembered, last time Dr. Jyoti had said that even I could give her that injection as it was easier compared to intramuscular administration.

There were a couple of things going around in my mind as we reached the hospital. First, visits to the hospital would have to be minimised as the pandemic situation was going on, and it would expose her to infections. Her immunity was already compromised due to chemo. There was no point in going to the hospital every time just for one injection. In addition, there was the fatigue while climbing the stairs every time. There was no point calling a nurse at home every now and then, as the chances of infection by coming in contact with an outsider were high.

I then decided to give that injection to her myself from then onwards. After reaching the hospital, I expressed my desire to Dr. Jyoti to administer the injection. She lauded my will and immediately took us to one of the compartments along with a nurse. The nurse explained the technique to fill up the syringe with medicine and to hold the injection at a proper angle to give it subcutaneously. I suppressed my fear for a bigger benefit and dared to take charge. Both of them were watching me. Deepika as usual was very cool.

She said, "I have full faith in you Sugat. Now don't let your hands shake!"

Looking at her confidence in me, I said, "Here we go!"

I went ahead and was able to do it without a hitch. I breathed a big sigh of relief.

Ever since I was in standard eight, I was sure that I was not going to become a doctor. The only reason was that I could not think of myself treating someone, or operating on someone, or even simply giving someone an injection. I had a feeling of discomfort and would worry about treating someone wrongly. Or what if because of my mistake someone suffered? After my tenth standard, many of my relatives tried convincing me to study medicine as I had scored well in school. Even my parents wanted me to become a doctor, but I was adamant on not going for it and going for engineering rather, which was my field of interest. I finally became an engineer, but who knew one day, destiny would make me face a situation where I had to do a medical duty of administering an injection, and that too to a person who was closest to my heart. The next week onwards till the end of chemotherapy, I was supposed to do the same at home every week.

So the injection was given. For the next three days, it was time to bear with aching joints and bones. Thankfully constipation wasn't a problem this time, but the nausea returned. The vomiting episodes, which had stopped around the fourth month, started again. She was not able to eat properly. It was necessary for her to do so, to keep the baby healthy and growing and to keep up her own stamina, but ensuring that she was receiving adequate nutrition was quite challenging.

Her pastime during these painful episodes was listening to her favourite motivational songs like '*Ud jaa ab teri baari hain*' and '*Dil ye ziddi hain*' from the movie *Mary Kom*. She would eagerly wait for day five when finally, she felt better for a couple of days at least, before the next chemo session. I requested Dr. Tushar to shift the chemo sessions to Saturdays, so that I wouldn't have to take leave from work. He permitted to shift, so henceforth, they were scheduled for Saturdays.

Meanwhile, it was time to meet our gynaecologist Dr. Aggarwal for pregnancy follow up. We were going to meet her for the first time ever since Deepika had been diagnosed with cancer. She had been briefed by Dr. Pranjali and Dr. Tushar. First of all, she did her routine checkup. Later on, as we spoke, she was sounding a bit compassionate. While the pregnancy checkup was fine, I felt that maybe she was feeling bad that she had waited for a long time before deciding to send us to get the lump checked by a breast expert. She told us that such lumps appear in fifty percent of her patients and go away on their own. Deepika was one in many thousands where it had turned into such a complication. She had just wanted to spare her the pain of getting the needle biopsy. She did not want to unnecessarily disturb the lump when it was anyway supposed to go away on its own.

We were, however, not upset or dissatisfied with her help and suggestions in any way. We still had the same trust in her, and carried on with our pregnancy consultations. She advised a sonography after a couple of weeks, during the twenty-eighth week. It was known as a growth scan as it was supposed to show us the growth of the baby so far. This scan was very crucial because it would tell us how much was the effect of chemo on the baby's growth.

When we were getting settled on our bed the next Saturday morning for the third chemo session, we saw a lady who seemed to be of the same age as Deepika. She was undergoing chemotherapy as well. It was her first session I suppose, as we had not seen her there before. After the chemo, when we were about to leave, Dr. Jyoti came to Deepika. She told us that the lady whom we had noticed was also suffering from cancer. She was still in shock about the diagnosis and had not yet digested the fact. She had been crying ever since she was admitted for chemo in the morning. Dr. Jyoti requested Deepika if she could have a word with her, as she was also going through a similar situation like Deepika's, except the fact that she was not pregnant.

While their short meeting was going on, I waited outside for Deepika. Once she came back, she told me how Dr. Jyoti told her about Deepika's case and requested her to calm down. She told her how Deepika had taken everything in a positive spirit in spite of being pregnant. Deepika too tried to console her and described her experience.

That day I came to know one thing indirectly, that all the doctors and nursing staff in the hospital had become great admirers of Deepika. Being pregnant, they anticipated her to be tense and fearful. They thought she would not tolerate the chemotherapy. But they were amazed at her spirit, grit and determination. They were full of praise for her, lauding her courage, and used her example to encourage and console others as well. In subsequent chemo sessions, some nurses, apart from their duty, would come to her personally, enquiring about her well-being.

Chemo effects on the baby and genetic testing

By mid-October, Deepika had completed four chemo sessions and she was twenty-eight weeks pregnant. It was now the time to go for the growth scan. I was a bit nervous while we were waiting outside our regular sonography centre, wondering about the impact of the chemo on the baby's growth. Deepika was called in by the radiologist. I followed, adhering to Covid appropriate protocol. It was the first sonography after the start of her chemotherapy treatment. I showed her file to the radiologist and briefed him about her case history so far. Accordingly, he started examining the baby.

It was an extremely worrying wait. We held our breath. And as we listened to the heartbeats of the baby on the machine amplifier, our own heartbeats raced, unlike the previous scans. The radiologist took his time to analyse everything thoroughly. Finally, after finishing the scan, he looked at us and said,

"The baby is alright!"

We breathed a huge sigh of relief. His words were music to our ears. He further went on and said that the growth of the baby was fine and corresponded with what was expected at that week. We hurried to our gynaecologist's clinic which was just a kilometre away from the sonography centre to show her the reports.

Dr. Aggarwal said the same thing after scanning the reports – the baby was doing fine. She explained that during pregnancy, there is an additional formation inside the mother's uterus apart from the baby, which is known as the placenta. Everything that flows through the blood vessels of the mother or everything she gets injected with, reaches the baby through this placenta. It filters the things that are not good for the baby. Probably in Deepika's case, the placenta was performing its job very well and had not let the chemo medicine affect the baby's growth so far. It was good news for us. However, the risk of preterm delivery was still present, as there were eight more chemo sessions left. Also, though so far the baby's growth was not retarded, there was no guarantee that it would be the same throughout the remaining term. We were hopeful and optimistic, as any other parents-to-be would be.

Dr. Tushar had said in the very first meeting that Deepika would lose her hair after two or three chemo sessions. But so far, even after four, her hair was intact. While it was a sweet jackpot for us, I was a bit surprised. But I decided not to discuss this with the doctor yet, and to go with the flow. It anyway would not make a difference. But, I asked one silly question to myself – If the hair was not falling, then was the chemo medicine working indeed?

I got the answer in the very next moment when I recalled what Deepika had been telling me since the last one week – that her tumour had shrunk considerably by about a third, and so there was noticeable relief from the pain associated with its giant size earlier. We informed the same to Dr. Tushar during his routine visit during the fifth chemo session. It had indeed shrunk due to the effect of the chemo medicines.

While the fifth chemo was going on, Dr. Pranjali too visited Deepika at the Daycare. She examined her for the tumour response and was satisfied with the effect of chemotherapy so far. She confirmed that we were going in the right direction. One important aspect that she came to discuss with us was genetic testing. Since it was a rare case of pregnancy with cancer, she did not want to leave any stone unturned in Deepika's treatment approach. Genetic testing is basically testing of a person's genes in order to check if there are some genetic mutations which led to breast cancer. In layman's language, genetic mutation means a change in the structure of a gene that might lead to the formation of a new variant which could, in turn, lead to the start of cancer. This variant of the gene can pass on from one generation to another. If this test was positive, we could conclude that she had got the cancer due to her genes and it was most probably inherited from her ancestors.

She insisted on getting this test done right then, as it would take another eight weeks for the report to be out. While it was not compulsory to do this test, she said that it would provide good inputs in hand, before we go ahead for the surgery after her delivery. At that point we had decided to have a partial breast surgery which only removes the lump and conserves the rest of the breast. This test, however, would be a big factor in confirming the type of surgery, i.e. whether to go ahead for a lumpectomy, or a mastectomy.

One more factor that needed to be taken into consideration while deciding whether to go ahead with this test or not was the cost associated with it, which was thirty-five thousand rupees. The next morning, I had a group call between myself, Pranali, Pratique and Vishal. I told them everything that was discussed with Dr. Pranjali regarding genetic testing. After listening to the inputs from everyone, I decided to go ahead with the test, even though it was costly. At some point, anyway, we would be looking at the probable causes of cancer to prevent it from coming back for the rest of her life. The best thing would be to rule out the possibility of the cancer being inherited, before the surgery.

6

CLIP INSERTION

The following Saturday, before starting the sixth chemo session, a nurse collected Deepika's blood samples for the genetic testing. There was a specialised genetic testing lab outside the hospital, where the samples were supposed to be sent and tested for the next eight weeks. Deepika was however not interested in knowing what these tests were all about or whether to go for them or not. For that matter, she was not even interested in knowing the medicines she was being given. She did not want to occupy even a single bit of her mind in knowing the details. She just knew that she had breast cancer and the overview of the treatment, and she was least interested to know anything beyond that. She left the details to me. She just wanted to take the medicines positively and patiently, and dedicate the rest of her time thinking and doing what was right for the well-being of herself and the baby. She wanted to keep away from all the stress and negativity in knowing the details. This was the best thing I could ask of her. Stress is an enemy of pregnancy. Especially when we knew that there could be a possibility of a premature baby, she did not want stress to be the reason behind her onset of labour pain. I agreed with her decision and hence willfully used to look at, scrutinise and take care of all the details during her treatment.

In the previous day's pre-chemo blood checkup, her haemoglobin or Hb level was down to around nine. It was her thirtieth week and Hb generally goes down around this time in normal pregnant ladies as well. In her case, chemotherapy had further lowered the level. This time again she was prescribed an iron injection. Dr. Jyoti, before giving her the injection IV, spoke to Dr. Aggarwal and Dr. Tushar and sought their approval. Everything was in sync between all the doctors, or rather the team of doctors.

Apart from genetic testing, Dr. Pranjali had discussed one more point. Deepika's tumour had shrunk considerably, and it was by then less than half of its original size. There was a possibility that by the time she finished her twelve chemo cycles, the tumour might vanish altogether. Even if it vanished, it didn't mean that she would not need surgery. The centre, or bed, of the tumour could still be active and once the chemo cycles would be over, it had the potential to regrow the tumour. So, there was a need to surgically remove whatever residual tumour was left after the chemo sessions and delivery, along with its bed.

In case the tumour vanished after the chemo cycles, then there would not be any reference for Dr. Pranjali to remove the tumour bed. Hence, there was a need to mark the bed immediately, when it was still there and could be seen on a sonography machine. To mark the bed, she was planning to insert a metal clip inside the tumour to be rested at its bed.

This clip would stay in till the surgery. At the time of surgery, it would be removed along with the residual tumour and some adjoining healthy tissues, so that there would be surety that the correct area was targeted and there would be minimal chances for the tumour to come back in future. Dr. Pranjali called us to the OPD for this, the following Wednesday.

Meanwhile, after completing six chemo cycles, there was a new issue. It was pain in her arms. Due to the intracath insertions and the blood sample needle pricks every week, there was swelling in both her arms at the pricking sites along with pain. She was advised by the doctor to apply an ice pack to get some relief. We tried to ease her pain by applying ice packs for two to three days after each chemo. By now, I was confidently giving her the filgrastim injection after each chemo at home. It would be painless sometimes, but at times it would hurt. She bore the pain stoically though. Along with her arms, both her upper legs also started aching due to the weekly injections. In short, from head to toe, her entire body would ache after each chemo for five days. Only the sixth day would bring some relief.

The pain in her arm due to the intracath was about to get worse. Dr. Tushar instructed Dr. Jyoti to use only her left arm as far as possible for inserting the intracath, and to leave her right hand unhurt at the moment. This was done to keep the right hand free for intracath later. After the surgery, no needle-pricks would be allowed throughout her lifetime on her left hand. This was because her tumour was in the left breast and during the surgery, after removal of the tumour, her lymph nodes in the left arm would also be removed to minimise the risk of the cancer coming back. Lymph node removal meant that she would be under constant risk of swollen arm due to infection. I will deep dive in the lymph nodes removal further while narrating about the surgery.

On Wednesday, as decided, we went to the hospital for the clip insertion procedure. Because of the chemo effect, as I said, the tumour was reduced in size. Now when it had become as small as a grape, there was something unexpected seen to Dr. Pranjali on the sonography just before the clip insertion procedure. Apart from the cancer tumour, she could now see the earlier known lump of fibroadenoma, that Deepika already had since her college days. It was very surprising that the earlier lump was still as it is. We were so far assuming that it had transformed into cancer during pregnancy. But the cancerous tumour was a different lump altogether that had grown adjacent to the earlier benign one.

During pregnancy, by the time we went for the first breast sonography, the cancer tumour was as large as an orange. Hence, the earlier small fibroadenoma was hidden and could not be seen by the radiologist. But now, when the tumour had shrunk, it could be seen again. Dr. Pranjali, however, said that there would not be any change in the plan, and during surgery, she would remove both the masses together. She then proceeded to insert the clip inside the cancerous tumour with the help of USG or sonography. The pain at the clip insertion site was another one that Deepika had to bear for a few days until it healed. Now that she had a clip inside her tumour to mark its bed, there was no need to worry even if the tumour vanished entirely.

7

SIDE EFFECTS OF CHEMO

Week after week, Deepika was experiencing a considerable amount of weight gain. She was thirty-one weeks pregnant and by now she had completed seven chemo cycles. There were two reasons for weight gain – one, pregnancy and another, chemotherapy. The previous week, Dr. Jyoti told us that chemo was also contributing to her weight gain as it is known to do so. A step was kept alongside her bed to help her climb and get down easily. Due to the weight, her stamina was declining further. Forget about climbing stairs, even walking around inside the house was sometimes a mammoth task for her.

While she was being patient with her chemo sessions, there were times when she'd be emotional and upset. Many times, she would let out a flood of tears.

"Why me?" she would sob, especially during the weekly peaks of pain.

A couple of times she screamed, while I was giving her an injection. It was not that she couldn't bear the pain, but she was fed up with bearing it, and was venting her frustration.

Adding to the frustration, there was nausea. As I said, she began to feel nauseous again after the start of chemotherapy. Although she had a tablet prescribed to chew whenever she felt sick, ironically she felt more nauseated after just smelling that tablet. Rather, throwing up would often make her feel better. I was by now habitual of swiftly grabbing a stool and putting it in the bathroom for her to sit on, as soon as she braced herself to puke, as it would often make her feel drowsy for some time.

She even lost the ability to feel hunger. She used to rest for many hours due to the pain and didn't realise when she was hungry. As the baby was inside her, she was supposed to eat something every couple of hours to keep up the energy. One day, she was resting for three to four hours and didn't realise that she was hungry. After she woke up, she was not able to get out of bed. She couldn't even stand, but she said that she was not hungry. I asked my mom to immediately serve her lunch and keep her plate ready, though she was still firm that she was not hungry. I somehow managed to get her up. She was very drowsy. With my support, she walked to the dining table. She was so weak that she was not able to even pick up the food and start eating, as her hands were shivering. Jayesh, who had been visiting, was at the table as well. We had to help her eat. While I was holding her, he took small portions and started feeding her. After five to six bites, she felt better and the shivering was gone. She managed to have the rest of her meal by herself. After lunch, she was able to walk by herself and felt better. A couple of similar episodes took place during that time. At that point she realised that she was not able to feel hunger. We then decided to keep her meal timings fixed, no matter whether she was hungry or not. The issue was sorted, but I was not happy at all. It was hard for me to control my tears, seeing my steady and strong wife reduced to this emotional state.

There was some relief in the meantime as Dr. Tushar gave her a break from chemo. It was the Diwali weekend and he said it was okay to take a break for a week as we were well within the planned schedule. It was a much-needed break for all of us. She was free from the chemo-related pain for a week. I was so glad that she could now joyfully celebrate Diwali. Since childhood, she loved to light diyas. I went out for Diwali shopping and got some new diyas for her. In the evening, the two of us literally sat in the balcony for a couple of hours in front of the diyas, feeling every bit of light. The atmosphere was wonderful and we blessed the doctor who had allowed us to celebrate the festival free of pain. Around this time, the family members collectively arranged a baby shower ceremony for her. We had initially thought this treatment and the side effects wouldn't allow us to have a ceremony and she would not be fit enough for it. Thanks to the break, it went off well and left us rejuvenated.

Deepika had completed thirty-two weeks of her pregnancy and it was time for another growth scan. Once again, we were about to see our baby and would come to know if the chemo had hampered its growth. As usual, both of us went in and our radiologist, Dr. Sachin, was ready with Deepika's case history in mind. This was a unique case for him as well. We waited with bated breath as we listened to the baby's heartbeats. Once he was done analysing, he reiterated that the baby's growth was fine this time as well. The chemo didn't seem to have hampered its growth so far.

The baby's weight, as calculated by the sonography machine, was 1.8 kilograms, which was within the normal range for this stage. There were a few more weeks to go. Dr. Sachin was very compassionate ever since he had come to know about the cancer. He said that he knew one of his relatives who had a premature baby weighing just 1.5 kg at birth. The baby was doing fine with medical help till it attained normal weight and started to grow on its own. Nowadays, medical science is very advanced, he assured us. Hearing this made us feel very positive and optimistic. Even if the baby would be born prematurely, we were sure that the doctors would be able to save him or her.

He further said that if the same normal growth continued, the baby's weight would increase approximately five hundred grams every two weeks from then on. We were happy that while chemo was treating Deepika's cancer well, it had not affected the baby's growth so far. We were optimistic that this would continue for the remaining eight weeks and the baby would be born fully matured in the end. Our gynaecologist Dr. Aggarwal too was happy to see the growth scan report. As usual, she said "I am so glad". These were her typical words every time she used to see something good. She was keeping an eye on the pregnancy and the baby's growth very closely. Usually the growth scan is prescribed every four weeks, but she asked us to get it done every two weeks from then onwards, to keep a close watch on the baby.

Although Deepika was suffering from a lot of pain due to chemo and the filgrastim injections, this one thing was keeping her going. She was being patient and bearing the pain with just one thought in mind – that the baby was doing fine. To distract herself from the pain, she continued watching the Gautam Buddha series even during the most painful times. By then she had almost completed watching it, and the last few episodes were left, in which Buddha was delivering sermons to his disciples. For me too, it was good to listen to them as she usually watched it with speakers on. We were getting teachings about the eternal truths of life, when life itself was making us go on a roller coaster ride. Everything was so relatable for Deepika that she started following his teachings. They helped her understand life better and to deal with her ongoing situation. His sermons were good for the baby as well. It was actually a proper garbh sanskar in progress.

After the Diwali break, it was time to resume the chemo sessions again. We were now habituated to the entire course. During the last few sessions, Deepika had experienced a feeling of warmth and suffocation while the chemo medicines were injected. Her increasing weight may have been the reason for this. Although the daycare facility was air conditioned, she still was in need of some flowing air. I requested the facility to arrange a portable fan for her. They did not have a fan handy, hence they used to arrange it from another department where it was not needed. It would take a lot of time to arrange one. A couple of times, the session was completed, but the fan never even arrived.

I remained very patient, but at one point I got very frustrated. During the eighth chemo session, I was in no mood to backtrack. I waited for a couple of hours after requesting for the fan. When the facility failed to arrange one, I went out to the nursing station. I knew that the daycare staff was honestly trying to get one from some other department, but couldn't get it. I located the office of the facilities manager of the hospital, and once inside her cabin, I did not hold back.

"Should it be so difficult to get a mere fan in a big hospital which boasts of so many facilities? Are you not serious about a patient's discomfort? If you cannot arrange one, let me donate a thousand rupees to this hospital to get one!" I blasted in anger.

Not sure whether it was my confrontation or the embarrassment caused to them, but a fan arrived beside Deepika's bed within the next fifteen minutes. And it was then supposed to remain dedicated for the daycare facility permanently. I realised that sometimes you have to cross the line to get things done.

Anyway, a week later, the month of December 2020 began. As usual, we were excited as December has always been a joyful month for both of us. Right from our relationship to our wedding, from our honeymoon to the UK trip – they had all taken place in December. The lockdown, which had been in place since March, had by now started yielding lockdown babies. Our baby was, however, due in mid-January. But with the ongoing chemotherapy and the possibility of preterm birth, we had a gut feeling that we could have a December baby. And don't know why, the date eighteenth kept coming to my mind. This date in the year 2010 marked the beginning of our relationship, and in 2015 we were wedded on that very date. The next major milestone of our life was also approaching. We were excited and were wondering to see if luck fulfilled another *panchvarshiya yojana* for us on the same date.

Deepika had by now completed ten chemo sessions. It was the first week of December and she was thirty-four weeks pregnant. It was time for another biweekly growth scan, as suggested by our gynaecologist. We were now less worried about the chemo hampering our baby's growth as things had worked very well until then. But this scan gave us other reason to worry. It was not the growth of the baby, but a loop of the umbilical cord which was wrapped around its neck. Our gynaecologist assured us that we still had time and the cord, many times, gets unwrapped automatically as the baby moves inside the womb. She told us that she also had experience of delivering a baby with the cord wrapped. This certainly made us feel relaxed about it. The next scan was after two weeks and we were hoping that the cord would get unwrapped by then.

The following Saturday, during her eleventh chemo session, once Dr. Tushar's visit and checkup was over, we had a good casual conversation with him. Being one of the top oncologists in Pune, he was a very busy man, who usually talked about nothing else apart from the treatment. But this time he spent some time with us enquiring about our well-being and how we were managing things. He was very happy with the way Deepika had co-operated and maintained her composure, despite all the pain and suffering. He gave her a pat on the back, which made her day. It was all going as per his carefully carved out and well-executed treatment plan. When asked about her hair being still intact, he said she should be happy that she was among the lucky five percent of patients, who do not experience hairfall. However, there were some other signs that the chemotherapy, which is in a way slow poison, was affecting her body. Her nails had turned dark by now. There were a lot of black spots on both her palms as well as tongue. Dr. Tushar confirmed that these were all effects of the chemo.

The following and last chemo cycle before delivery, he said, would be given only after discussion with our gynaecologist, once she analysed the growth of the baby and the proximity of the onset of labour pain. The chemo medicines and their side effects took at least five to six days to subside and he did not want her to go through the pain of chemo, while being in labour, which is a mammoth pain in itself. He asked us if we had any plans of a caesarean delivery or would we wait till the baby came on its own. Deepika told him that since the beginning, she was keen on the baby being delivered normally. Even the cancer could not destabilise her will. Our gynaecologist was very much in favour of normal delivery as well. She was supposed to compulsorily undergo breast surgery for the removal of the tumour after her delivery. Avoiding a caesarean meant avoiding one more surgery. Hence her will to have the baby delivered vaginally strengthened further.

After five days, while the last chemo related pain was subsiding, there were just a couple of days remaining for the eighteenth of December. I know, neither the date of delivery is in one's control, nor does it make any difference with respect to the happiness of having a child. But still, as we initially thought while trying to conceive, how cool it would be if we got our baby on the same date as our proposal and wedding, we were still thinking about it at the back of our minds.

And then suddenly, on the afternoon of seventeenth, Deepika started having intermittent contractions, which is usually the start of labour pain. A curiosity hovered over my head. I was like – really? It went on for some time. I started preparations for taking her to the hospital whenever needed.

After a couple of hours, however, the contractions stopped and she was back to normal. On the same evening, we watched the weekly YouTube video posted by noted gynaecologist Dr. Puranik, as a part of her series 'Pregnancy week by week'. We had been watching this series together for the past few weeks. In that week's video, Dr. Puranik talked about the same thing that had happened to Deepika that afternoon. What she experienced is known as Braxton Hicks contractions or false labour pain in layman's language. A few weeks before the actual labour starts, some women feel these contractions similar to labour pain, as the body gets itself ready for the actual labour pain.

"Ohh," we said in one voice after watching the video, laughing at our own childish expectations.

The next morning was our fifth wedding anniversary and tenth commitment anniversary - the 18th of December. How we wished that had yesterday's contractions been real, this morning we may have even welcomed our baby. The false labour, however, did not stop us from getting good news. Guess what? It was Pratique and Mayuri who became parents that very morning! I got a call from Pratique saying Mayuri had just delivered a baby boy. Ohh my... what magnificent news it was! We were elated! Apart from the king size happiness that we felt for our friends, for me, one more reason to be happy was that at least one of the two babies had been born that day. We would still be having double celebrations every year.

So our anniversary went off well, though we would have to wait for our baby for some more time. "Good," I said to myself as I gave it a second thought. The baby still wanted to grow inside Deepika so that he or she would be born healthy and we wouldn't need to worry later. The longer the baby stayed inside, the better with respect to its birth health and weight. If born on that day, it would have been a preterm baby as she was thirty-six weeks pregnant.

Nevertheless, we were about to meet our baby via the sonography machine as the next biweekly growth scan was due the next day. Baby's growth wasn't anymore an issue for us.

However, we were a little worried about that loop of umbilical cord wrapped around the baby's neck that we had seen in the last scan. But that little worry vanished this time, as the loop wasn't present any longer. It had unwrapped automatically, the possibility of which our gynaecologist Dr. Aggarwal had told us the last time.

There was another test we had to take. It was known as Non-Stress Test or NST. As the name suggests, it makes sure the baby is not under stress by monitoring its heart rate in continuation. We went to the Mother and Child Care hospital this time, as we were planning to have our baby there. The hospital, where the cancer treatment was going on, was a good multispecialty hospital and an excellent childbirth facility, but we planned to go to Mother and Child Care hospital for delivery instead, as it was comparatively cheaper. During all this treatment, we had to keep a close watch on the expenses, and save wherever we could, as the medical insurance was just about to get exhausted and we were supposed to bear all the further expenses from our own pocket.

Dr. Aggarwal would be handling the delivery, no matter which hospital we chose, as she was attached to both the hospitals. So, for the NST test, we went to the Mother and Child Care hospital. We wanted to have a look at the facilities there. During the test, a couple of belts were wrapped around her belly with the probes fitted on them to monitor the baby's heart rate. The results were normal. The hospital facilities were also fairly good. This test was just a trailer. During the time of delivery, those belts were supposed to be wrapped around her continuously to monitor whether the baby was under any stress and to act accordingly.

The previous day's growth scan had revealed that the baby's weight was approximately 2.7 kg, which was a healthy birth weight, even if the child would be born right at that moment. But we had to wait further. Dr. Aggarwal also explained to us the signs of the onset of labour and when we should get admitted to the hospital. Apart from contractions, the water breaking was also a sign that the delivery could happen anytime. So far, we were travelling to the hospital or doctor's clinic on our bike. She was always the pillion rider. But now we started travelling by cab. I did not feel sitting on a bike would be safe for her any longer.

"But I prefer sitting on the bike with you," Deepika complained.

I did not pay heed to her, obviously.

Day by day, as the pregnancy was progressing, Deepika was not able to sleep properly because of a couple of reasons. One, the weight of the belly and another, the movements of the baby. The baby used to kick every now and then. She'd wake up often during the night as the baby kicked and moved around. She was also supposed to wake up once at night to eat something to maintain her stamina. Bloating was also one of the reasons she had to stay awake till late at night, for which she had been advised to eat small meals at small intervals.

The chemo sessions were halted for our gynaecologist's go-ahead. One last session was remaining out of the twelve. Dr. Tushar had a discussion with Dr. Aggarwal regarding the same and he left it to her to decide the optimum timing of the last session. He did not want too much gap between the chemo and delivery as the absence of chemo medicine in the body would fuel the growth of the tumour once again. After the scan of week thirty-six, Dr. Aggarwal did not feel the proximity of labour pain for next seven to eight days at least. Hence she advised us to finish the remaining chemo session in a couple of days. Accordingly, on the 22nd of December, Deepika had her last chemo cycle out of the pack of initial twelve.

The urine test before this last chemo revealed Urinary Tract Infection (UTI) like results. However, she did not have any such symptoms. After looking at the report, to be on the safer side, I requested the pathology lab to let me provide them another sample of Deepika to rule out any misreading due to human error, as this was a late pregnancy stage and any complications now could result in serious health issues for the mother and the baby. I immediately came back home, asked her to give me another sample and went back to the lab with it. The findings were the same. I went ahead to meet their pathologist Dr. Prachi to discuss it. She was kind enough to send a person home for sample collection every time, saving Deepika the trouble to visit the pathology lab, as every week she was supposed to get her blood and urine checked before going ahead with a chemo session. Dr. Prachi told me that she had checked the urine sample herself and was very sure of the findings. However, she asked me to get the reports checked by our gynaecologist, as sometimes the UTI like result may be normal for this stage of pregnancy, and there could be another reason for these findings instead of UTI. As she said, Dr. Aggarwal did not suspect it was UTI. It was normal at this stage of pregnancy. Accordingly, she gave her go-ahead for the chemo session.

After the chemo session, again one last time before delivery, she was drowning in pain. One last time, I had to do my toughest task of the week – give her the filgrastim injection. The backache due to baby weight added to the overall pain. After five to six days, when the pain associated with the chemo subsided, we eagerly waited for our baby. The hospital bags for mother and the baby had been ready since a couple of weeks. It was almost the end of December and the end of the year. Deepika was thirty-seven weeks pregnant and she could now expect to have real labour pain any day. The suspense of whether it would be 2020 or 2021 was still hovering in the air.

On the morning of 31st December, she again started getting contractions. This time we waited for a couple of hours before concluding anything. But they were still on, so we went to our gynaecologist's clinic. For the first time, she checked her internally to see if the baby was ready to come out. She said that the baby had acquired its head down position, but it would still need some time. However, she asked us to let her know in case the contractions lasted beyond evening. They lasted intermittently till evening, but by the time we wished each other 'Happy New Year', they were gone. Luck was playing hide and seek with us. It was now confirmed that 2021 would be the year. New year, new beginnings.

On the 2nd of January, since the baby was not born yet, and Deepika had completed thirty-eight weeks, we went for another growth scan. This time the baby was fully grown, no umbilical cord loop around the neck and the weight as per the sonography was around 3.2 kg, which was already a healthy birth weight. Dr. Aggarwal was happy and she asked us to just wait for the baby to give an indication. Everything was under control. She said that the labour could start anytime, but we were by now bored with the waiting. The eagerness of seeing the baby in person was making the patience even worse. As the Hindi saying goes, '*Sabr ka fal mitha hota hai*', which literally means patience reaps a sweet fruit, we were just being patient. However, I was still fixated on dates. First of January was gone, second was gone, now I was thinking of the 10th of January.

10-01 would be a cool date of birth!

8

LABOUR PAIN AND DELIVERY

8th January 2021

On the morning of the 8th January, the contractions returned. We were anyway planning to visit Dr. Aggarwal that morning for a check-up. Once again, she checked her internally to see the chances of the baby coming out. As we know, right from week one till the labour starts, the baby rests and grows inside the uterus of the mother. There is a tiny cylindrical neck or tube of muscles known as cervix, which is the lower-most part of the uterus and it connects the uterus to the vagina or birth canal. During pregnancy, the cervix is filled with a plug of mucus that prevents outside bacteria from entering the uterus and thus keeping the baby safe from infections. This mucus plug breaks and flows out during early labour as a reddish or bloody discharge.

While Dr. Aggarwal was checking Deepika, she noticed this discharge, and told us that Deepika was in labour indeed and we had to get her admitted to the hospital for delivery. She advised us not to rush and to just go home calmly and come to the hospital in a couple of hours. After coming back home,

I informed our parents that we had to get her admitted. All four grandparents-to-be had turned up by now, to welcome the baby. There were happy faces all around at home as finally they would meet the little one. Meanwhile, Deepika took a warm relaxing shower, as she had to get ready for the toughest day of her life.

1:00 p.m. – As decided earlier, we all reached the Mother and Child Care hospital. Due to strict Covid protocol, not more than one person was allowed to go in with the patient. Not even till the hospital lobby. Hence, it was just the two of us who went inside, while our parents waited in the parking area with the hope that I would somehow convince the management to allow them to wait in the lobby at least. The good thing was – one person, who happened to be me, was not just allowed inside, but was also allowed to be by her side in the labour room during delivery as a birthing companion. Once inside, they immediately asked both of us to wear the hospital attire. While Deepika was waiting in the procedure room, I completed the admission formalities and deposited an initial amount of rupees fifty thousand at the cash counter. Our gynaecologist Dr. Aggarwal had already instructed the on-duty doctor to examine her on arrival. During the first examination, her dilatation was just one centimetre. Now, a non-medical background person would ask me – What is dilatation? Let me explain it in layman's language as her journey took all the efforts to make me half a doctor.

So basically, once the baby is fully grown, the body naturally starts giving contractions to the uterus. During each contraction, the baby is pushed out a little. Throughout labour, these contractions continue till the baby is pushed out of the body entirely. During early labour, while contractions begin, the baby starts its journey to the outside world by first proceeding to enter the cervix. This cervix then gradually opens up on each contraction to make room for the head of the baby to come out. The extent to which the cervix has opened is known as dilatation. It is measured on the scale of one to ten centimetres. Gynaecologists use this term to track the progress of the labour and act accordingly. Until six centimetres it is known as early labour and after that it is active labour. So Deepika was in early labour at that moment as she was one centimetre dilated.

3:00 p.m. – After spending some time in the procedure room for the initial examination, the staff shifted us to our room. Our parents were still waiting in the parking area. I spoke at the reception, but they said they followed strict Covid protocol and hence they wouldn't be able to allow anyone in, apart from one companion. I called my dad and asked them to go back home. I assured them that I'd call them again as soon as the delivery took place.

Dr. Aggarwal briefed us in the morning that she would be giving Deepika medicine to induce labour. Labour induction is done to stimulate the contractions of the uterus and to expedite the movement of the baby. Usually for first-time mothers, early labour is very slow and may last from a few hours to days. After some time, it becomes very difficult to hold on and deal with the pain. Hence to speed up the labour progress and to achieve normal or vaginal delivery, doctors take a call to induce labour. So in case of Deepika, after examining her, Dr. Aggarwal instructed the doctor to give her labour inducing medicines.

Once she settled down on her bed, a nurse came in with an NST machine and attached a couple of bands on her belly to monitor the baby's heart rate, and it would remain there until the delivery. A couple of other nurses came in to insert an intracath in her arm to inject the medicines. Of course, we had to use the already hurt left arm until the breast surgery, as the right arm had to be used post-surgery. Those nurses, who looked new to their job, messed up while collecting blood samples during the intracath insertion. I was watching them quietly, but at one point, when I could see blood scattering on the bed and floor, I snarled, "Just stop it, and send a good nurse in." They somehow managed to finish it off by themselves in a couple of minutes.

6:00 p.m. - Labour was induced, but the contractions were still not that strong. She was just waiting for them to become stronger. For a few minutes she'd rest, for a few minutes we used to talk, for a few minutes we watched TV, and for a few minutes she used to walk a few steps in between the contractions. The wait was tiring. Meanwhile, she saw through the window that it was raining outside.

"Rain in January?" she exclaimed. "See, even god is welcoming our child."

For a moment she was cheerful and forgot the pain. After some time, I got a call from a nurse that they were coming to collect her sample for a Covid test. Already fed up with so many tests, I asked them what was the need of a Covid test now? Neither of us had any symptoms. But she said that it was their protocol to perform a Covid test for each admitted patient. I did not want to argue and just wanted to focus on making Deepika feel cheerful during labour. There was no other person allowed and I was the only one with whom she could speak in person.

Dr. Aggarwal arrived in the meantime to check on Deepika. It was now an internal checkup every time to measure the dilatation. The checkup itself used to be very uncomfortable. She was still not more than 1.5 centimetres dilated. The doctor said that we had to wait till she began proper contractions. The patient is taken into the labour room only when active labour starts, i.e. when she was at least six centimetres dilated. While at home, everyone was expecting the baby to be born by the evening, but that didn't seem to be the case yet.

9:00 p.m. – Shortly after we finished having dinner, Dr. Aggarwal arrived once again in the room with an on-duty doctor. They asked us to put on our masks. What happened later was totally unexpected. Deepika's Covid report was out and she had tested positive! I felt the floor beneath my feet sliding. At that time, when Covid was fairly new, there was a lot of fear surrounding the health of a Covid positive person.

The vaccine hadn't been rolled out yet. Not even for healthcare workers. So far, Deepika was very calm and patient bearing her labour pain. But now, some fear was visible on her face. For the first time in a while, she began crying. She was fearful. Not for her, but for the baby. She feared she would contract the virus to the baby.

Being Covid positive was not the only worry. Another piece of bad news was waiting for us. The hospital told us that they wouldn't be able to carry out the delivery of a Covid positive patient there. They were planning to shift us to some other hospital. This was an even bigger shock for me. Deepika was in labour pain. We were already settled there with most of the luggage unpacked. I pleaded to the head of the hospital to make arrangements and have the delivery there itself. It would be a nightmare for us to shift her in the middle of labour pain elsewhere. The head, who was a gynaecologist himself, expressed his deep regret for not being able to allow us to be there. He said that it was a government rule that didn't allow them to have the delivery of Covid patients, as they did not have an isolation facility. There were other patients in the hospital as well, who could be at risk if he let us deliver our baby there. He assured all help from his side during and after the shifting.

10:00 p.m. – After all the doctors were gone, and it was just the two of us in the room, we had a long chat. Deepika, after her initial tearful reaction, gathered some courage and said, "Let us face whatever we are being served by destiny. Already the pregnancy was a roller coaster ride due to the cancer. How could we expect the delivery to go on without hurdles?"

"You are right, my dear. We will overcome this," I responded with a wary smile.

As usual, her courage gave me courage to tackle whatever was going to come our way. I made up my mind that I would ensure everything went smoothly and she should be bothered as little as possible during this transition. She was supposed to be shifted to the same multispecialty hospital where she had been undergoing her cancer treatment. It was the only hospital in the vicinity which had separate isolation wards and arrangements for the delivery of Covid patients.

9th January 2021

12:00 a.m. – A special Covid ambulance arrived to pick us up. Deepika, who was in pain and getting labour contractions in between, was brought down to the ambulance on a wheelchair. It was a big task to put her inside. The ambulance was just a van with a bed. It did not have any lifting facility or a ramp for wheelchair. On top of that, it was raining outside. A normal lady in labour would still be able to climb into the ambulance. But Deepika, having undergone so many chemotherapy sessions, had become very weak and she was not able to do it by herself.

The hospital nurse and I somehow managed to make her climb in and sit on the bed as she couldn't lie down. I thanked the nurses for their help, in spite of knowing that she was Covid positive, and then got inside and sat with her. While the ambulance was in motion, we were just looking out at the deserted streets, smiling at each other and at our situation, which was a perfect example of how things could turn turtle within a matter of minutes.

After reaching the hospital, she was temporarily kept isolated in the emergency ward until a Covid room was available for us. Till then, she rested on the stretcher. I completed the admission formalities. She was supposed to be given another dose of labour induction medicine by then, but we were still waiting for a room to be allocated. It had been more than an hour since she was on a stretcher and during her contractions, she was squirming in pain. She was Covid positive, hence the staff was a bit reluctant to attend to her, until the doctor arrived. She was pleading with me to shift her to the room as soon as possible. But I was helpless apart from assuring her that we would get a room soon. I was continuously visiting the emergency counter, every five to ten minutes, to try and get her a room as quickly as possible. Due to the limited number of Covid rooms, we were still waiting for someone to be discharged from one.

2:00 a.m. – Finally after waiting for a couple of hours, we got a room. The entire Covid ward was isolated, with a dedicated staff wearing protective gear. Once she settled on her bed, a nurse in this hospital again attached the NST belts to her abdomen to keep a watch on the baby's heart rate. Meanwhile, Dr. Aggarwal called me up and said that she had spoken to the on-duty doctor and briefed her about everything. She assured us that everything would be fine. Even though we were shifted to another hospital, Dr. Aggarwal was still our gynaecologist who would be delivering the baby. The on-duty doctor came a few minutes later and checked her internally. Her dilatation was the same – 1.5 centimetres. She started the medicines through IV and asked us to rest for some time now.

6:00 a.m. – After we had a brief nap, the doctor came in for an internal checkup once again. There wasn't any significant change in the dilatation. It was around two centimetres as the contractions too were not so intense. She asked her to freshen up and have breakfast so that she could start the labour induction medicines again.

7:00 a.m – While I was having breakfast, I got a call from home. Our families were concerned about her health, and also eager to hear the good news. But they were so far unaware about what had happened the previous evening. We decided not to hide anything from them so that even they would be cautious about Covid and avoid contact with others. I gave them the update and asked them to stay indoors as they prayed for Deepika's good health.

8:00 a.m. – Until then, the labour induction medicines that she had got were intravaginal. But, the induced contractions were not so strong. Hence her dilatation was slow. From then on, she was to receive the medicine through IV directly into the bloodstream. It was then expected that she would get comparatively intense and long-lasting contractions. Although she had tested Covid positive in the earlier hospital just a few hours ago, this time again a nurse came in to collect her sample for a Covid test. Assuming that it was their mandatory protocol, I just let them do it and didn't pay any attention.

9:00 a.m. – After the end of the shift, the on-duty doctor changed. The name of the doctor who came in was Dr. Bhavna. She took charge and details from the earlier doctor. Due to the IV medicines, Deepika started getting more intense contractions. She was now back in pain, which had slowed down for a few hours during all the shifting and resting. I was trying my best to divert her attention from pain as we were racing with time.

11:00 a.m. – Dr. Bhavna came in to check Deepika. Her dilatation was still two centimetres. After the checkup, she said that though contractions were there, her labour was not progressing. Deepika was aware of the fact that the early labour phase for first-time mothers is very long lasting, and she had prepared herself mentally to bear with it, as she was very keen on having the baby delivered normally. She had to anyway face breast surgery after the delivery, hence she did not want a C-section delivery. Dr. Bhavna, however, spoke about a probable caesarean delivery after her first checkup itself. We told her our intent of normal delivery and what we had discussed with Dr. Aggarwal throughout our journey so far.

Due to the weight and constant pain, Deepika was feeling suffocated. She was not able to breathe properly with a mask on. In spite of telling Dr. Bhavna, she said that Deepika should still wear it. She insisted that Deepika kept the mask on at all times. I didn't know why she was so firm, when she knew of the patient's discomfort. She was herself wearing a PPE kit and was fully protected. We were surprised by her behaviour. For the first time, we experienced such weird behaviour from a doctor.

2:00 p.m. - Deepika's contractions were fairly intense by now. They did not let her sit. She just had to lie down on her side. She was moaning badly as contractions came and went. It was time for another internal checkup. Dr. Bhavna said that dilatation was just two to three centimeters. In a rude and discouraging voice, she said that nothing can happen now and we'd just have to go for a caesarean delivery. I am not sure why she was in a hurry for a c-section and whose anger was she throwing at us, as she seemed very frustrated while speaking to someone on the phone. Citing a need for a caesarean delivery, she did not even allow Deepika to have her meal. She allowed her to have only clear liquids like water or juices. Later on, she even stopped her from drinking water.

Deepika was very upset with Dr. Bhavna's rude behaviour. She had already been in labour pain for more than twenty-four hours, and was still strong and bearing with it. All she needed was some kindness and encouragement from the doctor. But Dr. Bhavna was doing just the opposite. During her next visit after half an hour, I lost my cool and had an altercation with her. I asked her not to discourage Deepika and said we'd let Dr. Aggarwal decide what to do, and that she should just report the findings of the checkup to her. She retorted saying that she knew what she was doing, and went out of the room. It was highly unprofessional behaviour. For her, our case might have been a routine one, but for us, it was a maiden journey. The last thing we expected was this kind of rudeness. Probably she didn't know how Deepika's journey had been so far and how much was her endurance.

4:00 p.m – The contractions were now very intense, and slowly she was losing her bearing capacity. Dr. Bhavna's behaviour acted like a catalyst to lower down her pain threshold. Even the gap between the contractions was barely eight to ten minutes and a contraction would last for about a minute. During this minute, Deepika would moan with pain. The contractions enhancing medicine was continuously being injected through IV, with a steady and controlled increase in dose. Accordingly, her contractions were also increasing.

I would try to divert her attention from the pain since the previous day, but now, even that was not working. Many times, she scolded me in frustration while asking me to do something to make the pain stop. Dr. Aggarwal had told us during the earlier meeting at the clinic that she would use epidural to get her some relief. Epidural is an anesthetic injection that is given in the back near the spinal cord, in order to get some relief from labour pain. The tiny tube is retained at the site to administer doses of the medicine throughout the active labour pain. But she was just four centimetres dilated so far as per the latest examination, and we would have to wait for another two centimetres.

5:00 p.m. – I was trying different ways to keep her busy and distracted. I tried calling Dr. Jyoti from daycare who had been very friendly, supportive and encouraging throughout Deepika's chemo sessions. Since she was in the same hospital, I asked her if she could visit us for some time so that Deepika could have someone to talk to. Unfortunately, she was busy with patients. I even tried calling Pratique for a chat, as he is very good at keeping someone engaged while speaking. But Deepika was in no condition to speak on the phone. As it was a Covid ward, he or anyone else could not even come in for a visit.

In the meantime, a nurse came in to renew the IV medicine. She seemed to be a young eighteen or nineteen year-old girl whom we were meeting for the very first time. She saw how Deepika was groaning in pain. Instead of just leaving after the IV renewal, she stayed back and had a conversation with us. She asked her some questions like since when had we been going around, whether it was a love marriage or arranged? How we met each other, etc. She was trying her best to keep Deepika engaged in conversation during the contractions. In a way, she was a true caregiver.

6:00 p.m – It was time for another checkup and another encounter with Dr. Bhavna. Deepika was fed up with those internal checkups by then. Initially they were just uncomfortable, but now, after more than a dozen times in the last twenty-four hours, they were rather painful. But as they say, pain yields gain. This time she was six centimetres dilated.

It was now time to take her to the labour room where all the arrangements for delivery would be present. Her early labour was finally over and she was now in active labour which lasts for a lesser duration. I spoke to Dr. Aggarwal over the phone, and conveyed to her that she had borne enough pain so far, and we wanted her to be given an epidural, as using epidural doesn't usually involve any risk to the mother or the baby.

While she was being shifted to the labour room, I followed her. However, I was stopped at the door and the nurse there told me that I was not allowed inside. This was again an unpleasant surprise for me. Deepika desperately wanted me to be by her side. I wished the same as well. She had even asked me to make a promise a few days ago, that I should be present beside her while welcoming our baby.

"I can bear the pain to any extent if you're by my side," she had said.

I was fully committed to my promise. But unlike the previous hospital, this hospital was not allowing the companion in. For some time, I waited outside on a couch, thinking that I should not be a Covid threat to someone else. But I knew I had to be in there with her. I could feel her pain, and visualised how she must be desperately waiting for me. She didn't know that I was not allowed. We hadn't even said good bye to each other, as we were assuming that we would be together all through.

About half an hour later, Dr. Bhavna came to me asking for the Covid positive report. I showed it to her on my mobile phone. On asking why she wanted it, what she said took me by surprise. A pleasant one this time. She told me that Deepika had tested negative in that day's Covid test. She just went away without expressing anything, but I was very happy. I didn't know how it happened, but I safely assumed that the previous report was false. This bit of news also gave me the courage to get up and fight for going in, to be with my love.

7:00 p.m – I went ahead near the entrance of the labour room, and spoke at the nursing counter which was just beside the door. I asked them why they were not allowing me to go in. Suddenly a lady, who was another doctor on duty I suppose, appeared from nowhere and confronted me. She asked me why I was creating trouble. I replied that I did not have any intention to create a scene. It was a special case, my wife was suffering from cancer, and she was in a lot of pain. She wanted me beside her. I told her that I would just stand away from the bed and wouldn't get in the way. It was allowed in so many other hospitals, then why not there? I also said that in case the doctor decided to perform a caesarean at the last minute, then I would simply come out. She was, however, in no mood to calm down. Probably she had a preconceived notion about me, thanks to my verbal spat with Dr. Bhavna earlier that afternoon. I decided not to escalate the argument with her any further.

Rather, I chose another effective way. Thankfully, I was well aware of 'where to go for what' and 'how to get things done' in this hospital as it had almost been our second home for the past three months. I spoke to Dr. Aggarwal on the phone and called up the admin manager of the hospital there. By the time she arrived, I wrote an application on a piece of paper seeking permission to be allowed inside the labour room. I wrote down everything that could get me the permission. The manager was very polite. When she arrived, she spoke to me, and asked me the issue. I told her everything. She also spoke to Dr. Aggarwal on the phone and granted me permission immediately. Even Dr. Aggarwal knew from the beginning that we wanted to be together during delivery. While I offered her the handwritten application letter, she said that it was not needed. She instructed the nursing station to provide me with the labour room attire and let me go in.

8:00 p.m. – I was delighted to be inside. Deepika gave me a big smile when she saw me coming. I told her that I had kept my promise. I was with her, and now she should just focus on her contractions, I told her. By this time, the anaesthesiologist also inserted and fixed an epidural tube on her lower back with one shot of medicine already administered. Coming back to her pain and contractions, she was still in a lot of pain, even after the epidural. The contractions were very intense. The dilatation was about seven to eight centimetres. Dr. Aggarwal was supposed to come in when it would be ten centimetres. It was now expected to reach ten very soon.

Meanwhile, around 08:30 p.m., I got a call from the earlier hospital. They asked me for my UPI number, and as a refund, they immediately paid back the full amount that I had deposited with them the previous day. It was a good gesture from their side and saved me a trip later to claim a refund or have any arguments. Probably they came to know that Deepika was tested negative in the latest RT-PCR test report here. Yesterday what they did was a rapid antigen test, which is not so reliable. It must have yielded a false positive result, based on which they denied her to deliver there.

On the other hand, I was also continuously getting calls from home as well as from Pratique, Vishal and all our other friends. Everybody was eagerly waiting to hear the good news, but no one knew about our ordeal so far. I was honestly not thinking about the baby anymore. All I wanted was that my wife should be out of this pain as soon as possible.

9:00 p.m. – It was time for duty change. I breathed a big sigh of relief as Dr. Bhavna's duty got over. The next doctor who arrived for the night shift was Dr. Prajakta. The moment she came in, she brought along positive vibes. She was very polite and compassionate towards Deepika. Once again, she prepared herself for bearing another round of pain. Dr. Prajakta spoke to both of us and gave her a lot of encouragement. She said that she would assist Dr. Aggarwal in the delivery, and that we shouldn't worry. They would do their best to ensure everything was carried out smoothly. Deepika was nine centimetres dilated at the first internal checkup by Dr. Prajakta.

I asked her if she could eat something. Dr. Prajakta was surprised that she had not eaten anything yet. I told her that she had not been allowed to by the earlier doctor. She asked me to feed her some juice or else she would get out of energy at the time of pushing. I immediately arranged a juice for her as she was thirsty and hungry since the afternoon.

The nurses and the housekeeping staff soon started preparations for the delivery. They were arranging all the instruments in the sequence of their needs. Even the paediatric nurse and doctor were ready inside and they were preparing the things that they would need to take care of the baby immediately after the birth. The anaesthesiologist, who was taking care of the epidural administration, was also present. I sat on a chair beside her till the actual delivery procedure started. In the meantime, Deepika was injected one more dose of epidural through the tube. Epidural is supposed to block the pain of the person in labour while the person can still feel the pressure and push. But in her case, in spite of giving epidural, the pain had not reduced. She was somehow bearing with it. As time passed, she was becoming impatient. She had been in labour for the past thirty-five hours. I was helpless at Deepika's painful plight. Her body had already been subjected to so much of pain due to chemotherapy, and then this. I wondered why on earth should someone be made to suffer such an immense amount of agony.

10:00 p.m - Finally she was ten centimetres dilated. That meant her cervix was now fully open and her body would soon push the baby towards the vagina or birth canal. It would still take a couple of hours or so for the baby to come out. At this point, Dr. Prajakta called Dr. Aggarwal and asked her to reach the hospital. She finally reached and by the time she got ready, all the concerned staff had gathered at Deepika's bed for the final proceedings. Deepika felt a bit relieved to see Dr. Aggarwal, as she was now sure that this prolonged pain would soon end. I was standing isolated at a corner beside Deepika's bed, close to her near the head, so that I didn't disturb the people in action. It was 11:45 p.m. We had a chat with Dr. Aggarwal for a few minutes, before she gave a final look at the position of the baby's head. While exchanging a lighter note with her, I told her that we were anyway thinking of the 10th of January from a few days as the D day, and after five minutes the tenth would start.

Dr. Prajakta told me that even Madam's (Dr. Aggarwal) birthday was on the tenth. "Ohh! Great!" I exclaimed, "So both the baby and the birthing doctor will share the same birth date."

10th January 2021

12:00 a.m. – Dr. Aggarwal and Dr. Prajakta started the proceedings. Since Deepika was fully dilated, she was going through the second stage when the baby is pushed inside the birth canal and finally comes out. The flow of contraction enhancing medicine was now gradually on the rise. Accordingly, Deepika was getting stronger and more painful contractions. Both the doctors were keeping a watch on them, as the baby can only be pushed out during a contraction. During the rest period in between, the internal muscles relax and you cannot push. When they saw she was getting the next contraction, Dr. Prajakta pronounced loudly, "Come on Deepikaaa... *Push!*"

As she was now pushing in pain, her moaning turned into screaming. *In how many pushes does the baby come out?* was the question in my mind, as I wanted her to be free of it soon. But it wasn't a quick process either. For a couple of times, even I cheered for her, while she was gathering all of her power from within to push. She kept pushing one after another contraction. At one point, she was tired. Probably her stamina was going down as she hadn't had any food for fifteen hours. Dr. Aggarwal was motivating her to push with all her strength. She said that she could touch the baby's head. All she wanted was that Deepika should push harder. "One good solid push is all we need," she said as Dr. Prajakta cheered for her during every contraction.

1:00 a.m. – It had been an hour since both the doctors had been trying to get the baby out, but their efforts had not yielded any fruit. Deepika was tired of pushing. Her stamina was going down with every push. The baby's head could be seen, but it was stuck in the birth canal. Its heart rate was being continuously monitored by the NST machine. Had the baby's heartbeat increased beyond a certain limit, then Dr. Aggarwal would have had to take a decision to go for a caesarean at that very moment. But the baby was still fine, in spite of being stuck.

They then started trying alternate ways. A couple of nurses gathered on either side of her bed and started pushing the baby downwards externally during the contractions. Dr. Aggarwal made a small incision to widen the vaginal opening to help the baby come out easily. It is a normal practice and the cut would be later stitched after the delivery. At this point, I got away from the bed and stood at a corner of the room to let all of them do their job without any disturbance. Deepika was fully focused on pushing. When that too didn't seem to work, Dr. Aggarwal instructed the staff to get her the instruments of a vacuum cup. It was 01:20 a.m. I was now nervous. An hour ago, everything was looking under control, but now things were starting to lean towards a caesarean delivery. I was just hoping that somehow the baby should slip out. Deepika had come a long way. She would have opted for a caesarean earlier itself, without going through such a painful ordeal.

Anyway, Dr. Aggarwal fixed the vacuum cup at the head of the baby, who was stuck, but could be seen from outside. During the contractions, Deepika was supposed to push while the doctor would pull the head out with the vacuum cup. So far, I had seen such a delivery just in the movie *3 Idiots*. But here I was watching it live. Both the doctors were trying to motivate and cheer her. She, too, was not willing to give up in spite of getting tired. It had been almost forty hours now, and she was still determined to deliver normally.

The last dose of epidural had been given a while ago. But it didn't make any difference to the pain. She did not want it anyway. The flow of contraction medicine was increased once again. But now, for some reason, the contractions started lowering in intensity. Even the doctors were clueless why she was not getting contractions in spite of the medicine.

Dr. Prajakta looked at Dr. Aggarwal and asked, "Where are the contractions?"

One good push was all they needed. Both of them tried pulling the baby out by vacuum cup several times, but to no avail. Deepika was still optimistic in spite of being heavily wounded.

It was 01:35 a.m. Both the doctors discussed something for a minute and then Dr. Aggarwal came to me. She told me that they had tried a lot of different ways, but the baby was stuck, and that they had to now proceed with a caesarean delivery. I was okay with anything, but a bit worried because the head had already reached the birth canal and it would be a bigger caesarean cut now. Plus, the cut that they made at the vaginal opening had to be stitched. But I had no option. I gave a free hand to Dr. Aggarwal and asked her to do whatever she felt necessary. I could not see Deepika in such a situation anymore. I signed the undertaking form right there, and gave them the permission to take her to the operation theatre.

01:40 a.m.– Dr. Aggarwal went back to Deepika to get her sign as well on the undertaking form. She said, "Beta, you have tried a lot, but you are tired and not able to push harder. Let us proceed for a caesarean now. You can't do it..."

That's it. These words provoked her to give it a try once again. The doctor said it unknowingly, but she didn't know that it was Deepika's nature to take up the challenge and accomplish it by hook or by crook when someone says she can't do something. When Dr. Aggarwal told her she couldn't do it, she replied with confidence, "Doctor, before I sign the form, let me try one last time. Just one last time!"

Upon her request, both the doctors and nurses took their positions once again. It was literally like one last ball remaining and six runs were required. She had to hit a sixer. After a couple of minutes, she indicated to the doctors that she was getting a contraction. And then, gathering all of her energy at once, screaming out as loudly as she could, she pushed with all her might. The baby's head, which had been stuck, just slipped straight out. After the head was out, Dr. Aggarwal pulled the baby out of her entirely. The baby was born. Deepika had indeed hit a sixer on the last ball!

01:45 a.m. – After rubbing the baby's back a couple of times, it started crying, and all of us breathed a big sigh of relief with tears of happiness rolling down my eyes. They handed over the baby to the paediatrician, after cutting the umbilical cord. The paediatric staff rested the baby on their fully equipped table. To be on the safer side, they connected oxygen supply to the baby, as it had come out from prolonged labour. I was just standing next to it. After peeping through the nurses around the baby, I finally got a glimpse. Looking at Deepika, I exclaimed, "It's a boy!" She was so happy after hearing that. It was an emotional moment for both of us. She hadn't seen the baby so far, but I indicated to her from a distance, that he was doing fine. She smiled again.

02:00 a.m. - The baby was delivered, but the delivery was not over yet. The third stage of labour is the delivery of the placenta. As I mentioned earlier, placenta is formed along with the baby inside the uterus, which provides nutrients to the baby from the mother, and also filters waste products from baby's blood. It is detached from the uterus immediately after the birth, and needs to come entirely out of the body, else there could be chances of severe infection. So, after the baby was born, Deepika was still getting mild contractions to expel the placenta. After handing over the baby to the paediatrician, Dr. Aggarwal continued to look after Deepika, and the placenta was finally out around twenty minutes after the baby's birth.

On the other hand, our newly born son was being taken care of by the paediatrician in the same room. He said that since the baby had undergone prolonged labour, he was under stress and was having difficulty in breathing. Citing these reasons, they were shifting him to the NICU which was located in the same hospital. My focus was now divided between both my loved ones. A bit worried about the baby's health, I could not stop myself from escorting him till the NICU with the staff. I told Deepika that I was going with the baby to get him settled at NICU. She asked if he was doing fine. I reassured her that he was fine, and that I would be back soon.

I then went ahead and followed his portable incubator trolley. I walked with him till wherever I was allowed. The person on the NICU counter gave me the admission slip and I completed the admission formalities for the baby. His birth weight was a little less than three and a half kilos which was a healthy birth weight. After getting permission from the doctor there, I went inside to meet him. He had calmed down by now and was sleeping. There were a lot of wires and tiny tubes attached to his nose, mouth and chest. I asked the nurse about his health. She said he was recovering from the labour stress now and would be fine in a day or two. There was no need for us to feed the baby. He would be fed formula milk and the nurse would take care of that till he would be handed over to us. I was relieved from the baby point of view, as I was not supposed to come back there till the morning at least. Now once again, I headed back to the labour room.

3:00 a.m – While walking, I felt at ease assuming that the long battle was finally over. However, once I reached the door of the labour room, I could still hear Deepika's moans and loud screams. I was not expecting this at all. I thought that by now, the small incision that the doctor had made earlier to assist the baby come out, must have been stitched, and she must be resting. But her plight was still far from over. The nurse told me that stitching was still going on. Half an hour had passed since I was gone. I again fell deep into the same well of worry, as I was yet to meet the doctors to ascertain what might have happened. I just showed my face to her to let her know that I was back. Dr. Prajakta and Dr. Aggarwal were stitching her up.

In spite of being neck dip in pain, the first thing she asked me, as soon as I went in was, "How is our baby?" I told her that he was absolutely fine and sleeping. Her agony made me too distressed to sit inside and she read it from my face. I just told her that I would wait outside and sat on a chair. For the next half hour, it was still going on. I was tearful thinking of the torture she was going through. I just wondered why on earth did only women had to go through this, and why couldn't I share her misery The sooner I was hoping for the ordeal to come to an end, the longer it was taking. For the first time, a question struck my mind – "How much pain is too much pain?"

Finally, the screams stopped and Dr. Aggarwal came outside. She told me that the delivery was all okay, but since the baby's head was stuck in, it came bursting out tearing everything at the final push. There were internal tears all along the baby's path in the birth canal. Maybe because her body was already brittle and worn out due to the chemotherapy, the internal tissues could not withstand the pressure. The doctor further said that they had to stitch everything inside, layer by layer and then finally stitch the outside cut that was made manually. She had more than a hundred internal stitches, and they stopped counting after hundred. Also, she had lost a lot of blood. I asked her if there was any reason to worry. She said that Deepika would be injected with a couple of units of blood the next day and should be fine. On the stitches front, she said that they would need some time to heal and that she would prescribe some pain relief medicines for the initial few days.

4:00 a.m – While we were discussing this, Dr. Prajakta too finished the final bits and came outside. She heavily lauded Deepika's endurance and her pain bearing capacity. She said that it was rare to see such tolerant patients. I thanked both of them from the bottom of my heart for what they had done that night, and expressed to them that they were real gods for us. I told Dr. Aggarwal that we would always remember her on our son's birthday, as it was her birthday as well. At last, I wished her a happy birthday before she left the hospital.

After speaking with the doctors, I went in to check on Deepika and how she was doing. Finally, after forty-two hours of a marathon fight with pain, she came out winning. When I went in, she was still smiling, even though all of her energy was literally squeezed out of her. I asked her what she was made up of, that she was smiling in spite of bearing all that torture. Very politely she replied, "Don't forget that I am an army man's daughter! We just never surrender!" I got my answer.

05:00 a.m. – She was now allowed to eat anything that she wanted. Just that it should be easy to digest. She was strictly advised to keep constipation at bay for a few days, as it would complicate the situation around the stitching area. I ordered a couple of sandwiches right there in the labour room as I was hungry too. After a long time, finally we ate! Now, when everything was finished, I took a calm breath and informed everyone on calls and messages about the good news. Needless to mention, everybody was elated. At around five, she was shifted back to the room with the intracath still in her hand to keep the medicines on. Now both of us badly needed just one thing – sleep!

9

MILK SUPPRESSION

After sleeping for a couple of hours, I woke up to someone knocking on the door. It was Dr. Jyoti, whom I had called up the previous day while Deepika was in labour pain. She was very happy for us. The moment she came in, she hugged Deepika, as she couldn't come the previous day, being busy with patients. However, she made it a point to visit us in the morning. I briefed her about the labour story. From the beginning of the treatment until that moment, she had witnessed every stage of Deepika's fight. We had a nice chat after which she had to head back to her daycare duty. Once she was gone, I went down to meet the baby at the NICU after wearing Covid appropriate gear. It was a happy sight as he was sleeping peacefully. I asked the nurse how he was doing and she said he was fine. With her permission, I clicked a couple of pictures of him for Deepika to see.

Our parents too were eager to meet her and the baby. We hadn't seen them since the last couple of days. But they were not allowed inside as we were in the Covid ward. Deepika had tested negative in the previous day's RTPCR report, so I went to the nursing counter and asked them when they would shift us to the regular maternity floor, which had very good and spacious rooms, a speciality postpartum care, and most importantly – family was allowed to visit. But, the shifting was still a distant possibility. They said that they would retake her sample for the RTPCR test, and would shift her to the maternity floor only after that day's test would be negative. The hospital was big enough to have the RTPCR test facility right there within the premises. The report would be out in five to six hours, unlike the one done elsewhere, which took around twenty-four to forty-eight hours. Hence, I didn't bother much and asked them to collect the sample as soon as possible as we were eagerly waiting to be shifted.

Throughout the day, a lot of energy and pain relief medicines were given to Deepika. Around the afternoon, as instructed by Dr. Aggarwal, a bag of blood was connected to her IV line. Deepika told me that while the post-delivery proceedings were going on, she could see a lot of cotton rolls stained with blood. So much that a couple of bins were filled up and still the stitching work had not been completed. Usually, after normal delivery, a significant amount of blood loss happens, but in her case, the internal tears were a huge addition. A hundred plus stitches meant it was far beyond the scale that I could imagine. Her haemoglobin, which thankfully increased to eleven point something later in her pregnancy, was down to seven that morning. Hence, she was to receive a couple of blood units externally to maintain her vitals.

Around seven in the evening, her Covid test report was out and it was negative again. Now it was beyond any doubt that she did not have Covid, so I started pushing the staff to shift her to the maternity room. We were shifted within an hour. The room was very spacious and lavish, almost like a plush hotel room. It instantly changed our moods. Of course, great service and facilities come at a great cost. That's the reason we had chosen the other hospital earlier, but our destiny was not in a mood to let us settle with anything ordinary. It was good to be a part of the normal world again. For the past two days, both of us had been in an isolated bubble. We were elated to finally be able to meet our parents.

Except for me, no one had met the baby yet. It would be allowed for others only after the baby was handed over to us. Deepika was very eager to meet him, but she couldn't walk due to the stitches. Forget walking, she was not even able to stand. She was confined to the bed. Even while switching sides, her stitches would hurt. Hence, she had to settle with just the pictures of the baby for the time being.

The next morning, she insisted that she wanted to go and meet the baby. I asked the nurse to arrange a wheelchair for her. With a lot of added cushioning, we managed to shift her to the wheelchair and took her to the NICU. She and a nurse were the only two allowed to go in. Her joy knew no limits when she saw our little one for the first time. While I was the first one to see him, she was the first one to touch him. It was a very happy mother-baby reunion.

But... yes, there was a 'but' here as well. In the very next second, her tears of happiness turned into tears of sorrow, when she looked around her. The mothers of most of the babies were breastfeeding their newborns. Deepika, who had undergone so many chemotherapy sessions just a few days back, was barred from breastfeeding. Though she had been mentally prepared for it, now when she was actually facing the situation, it was very difficult for her to control her emotions. She was broken from inside. She made a kissing gesture towards our newborn and immediately requested the nurse to take her out from there.

After coming back to the room, I tried to console her.

"Don't you worry, our baby will be absolutely fine. Medical science has grown a lot. It will not let our baby be deprived of his nutritional needs. You know that formula milk almost mimics the mother's milk in terms of nutrition."

It was not that she didn't know all of this. She knew that the baby's nutrition would be taken care of. But then, a mother's heart is a mother's heart.

It was not just about her milk not being allowed for the baby, but her milk production was supposed to be suppressed altogether. Her breast surgery was planned in a few days, hence Dr. Pranjali had already coordinated with Dr. Aggarwal to give her lactation suppression medicine as soon as she delivered, so that the milk should not form at all. It was a tough, but necessary call for us to give our consent to. Even if there wasn't any surgery, the milk production still needed to be stopped.

If not, then it could lead to blockage of milk ducts, formation of lumps, which could further lead to infection of the breasts. Hence, she was on the milk suppression medicines ever since she delivered.

In the afternoon, Dr. Aggarwal visited her for a checkup. While the stitching area appeared normal to her, the one thing that bothered her was the blood count. In spite of giving a unit of blood, her haemoglobin was still going down according to the latest reports. This was not good. She was suspecting that some of the internal stitches might have ruptured and there was some internal bleeding. Deepika was once again taken to the labour room for a detailed internal checkup. Dr. Aggarwal, before going in, spoke to me. She made me aware that they would be doing a speculum examination, which means they would check up the birth canal with the help of an observation device. In case she had internal bleeding, some of the stitches would need to be opened to reach there and then they had to be re-stitched. It was scary to mere imagination. Deepika's screams were still fresh in my ears. I prayed fervently that she wouldn't have to go through it again.

Co-incidentally and thankfully, it was again Dr. Prajakta on duty who was assisting Dr. Aggarwal for the checkup and any rework if needed. After the checkup, they didn't find any bleeding from the external layer of stitches. However, to rule out hematoma, they decided to get a sonography of the region done. Hematoma is a collection of blood below the skin when there is internal bleeding. It would be visible on the sonography machine if it was there. While Deepika was being taken to the radiology department, both the doctors followed her to personally look at the sonography and make sure there was nothing suspected left out. As usual, I followed the convoy till wherever I was allowed.

The sonography revealed that there was no hematoma and hence no internal bleeding. I, along with both the doctors, breathed a big sigh of relief. Dr. Aggarwal told me that there was no need to touch the stitching and it was all fine. There must have been a timing error on the blood reports. The sample must have been collected before the blood transfusion. She asked the nursing station to transfuse another unit of blood to her that day and collect the sample the next day. Also, she was supposed to be strictly monitored for any infection around the stitched region. She had also been receiving infrared light therapy for faster healing of stitches.

Once I was free from this potentially disruptive, but well averted mess, I let Deepika rest inside the room and went to the NICU to check on how the baby was doing. It was more than thirty-six hours that he had been in the NICU. When I went in, he was getting blue light therapy to avoid jaundice, which is quite common in newborns. I spoke to the paediatrician there and asked him when they would be handing over the baby to us. He said that the baby was still under observation. Although he was no longer under labour stress, his oxygen saturation was still not normal without external oxygen support. They were monitoring him for the feed tolerance as well. So far, he was well tolerating the formula milk, but they had to continue observation that entire day at least. I pushed myself to believe that he indeed needed the NICU care even though he was apparently looking fine. I let them do what they wanted to their satisfaction. I did not want to take any risk with the baby, who had already had his share of sufferings so far.

The next morning finally brought some relief to us. We got four pieces of good news. First, I spoke to the Head Paediatrician Dr. Tambe and he was satisfied with the response of the baby to feeding as well as oxygen saturation. Also, the baby had not developed any signs of jaundice. Hence, he was okay to be handed over to us in a couple of hours. Secondly, Deepika's blood reports that morning had shown significant rise in the haemoglobin level, which was a good sign for her recovery. By now, she was also able to walk a few steps by herself. The third was that Dr. Aggarwal visited her in the morning and after all the checkup, she was ready to discharge her by the evening. That meant we would be going home with the baby on the same day.

Our parents gathered in the room to welcome their grandson. They hadn't seen him in person as yet. At around half past twelve, the baby was brought into the room by a nurse. It was a very happy moment for all of us. A big fancy blue tag was pasted on our door which read, "IT'S A BOY". Everyone was lining up to take him in their arms. Deepika, who had barely walked a few steps in the morning, started moving as if nothing had happened. She took turns to cuddle him as much as she could. By then she had gathered her strength and was prepared for not being allowed to breastfeed. Rather, she decided to focus on ensuring to fulfill his nutritional needs herself in the best possible way. The nurse, before leaving, explained to us how to make the formula milk and how to feed the baby. She fed him in front of us as a demo.

After some time, Dr. Jyoti came in to meet Deepika again. She was happy at the way Deepika had borne everything and successfully delivered a healthy baby. A few minutes later, Dr. Pranjali came in to meet her as well. She congratulated us on the arrival of our baby. Dr. Aggarwal had already briefed her about how the delivery happened. Also, she examined Deepika to check the tumour.

The fourth piece of good news was conveyed to us by Dr. Pranjali. The reports of the genetic testing, which was done in November, were out and it was negative! That meant she did not have mutations in her genes as a cause of cancer. In layman's language, her cancer was not hereditary. If the report would have been positive, then there would be a greater chance for the cancer to relapse. We would have had to live with that fear for a lifetime, because genes cannot be changed. Even the line of surgery would have been different in that case and it would make more sense to do a complete mastectomy. Maybe to one or both of the breasts. But now, a lumpectomy would be performed and only the tumour area would be removed. Negative genetic testing report was a huge relief for us.

Before leaving for home in the evening, our baby received his first set of vaccines. A paediatrician visited our room and performed a couple of quick tests. One was a hearing test and the other one was a vision test. He told us that both the senses of the baby were fine. Finally, after the ordeal that Deepika had faced, we headed back home with our little bundle of joy. Childbirth is indeed a miracle and women are blessed with this ability. Ever since the delivery, and especially after watching it live, respect for women in my heart has increased by a thousand-fold.

10

BABY DUTIES AND SLEEPLESS NIGHTS

Mom went back home before us and she made all the preparations to welcome the baby. Deepika has a special liking for diyas or oil lamps since her childhood. Her name itself is derived from them. That's why Diwali is her most favourite festival. During the previous Diwali when she was in her third trimester, she expressed her wish for the baby to be welcomed at home by lighting diyas. Mom did exactly the same. When we reached home with the baby in her arms, a grand welcome, with glowing diyas was waiting for us. It was the second Diwali of the season.

Once we were inside, we started feeding him immediately. There was no scope for rest. He was supposed to be fed every couple of hours. Since Deepika was in the recovery stage, she had to rest as much as possible. The doctor said that the outer stitches would heal in about ten to fifteen days, but the internal ones would need a couple of months to heal completely. It was now me, along with both the grandmothers, who were taking care of feeding the baby. At least two of us were needed at a time. One would prepare the milk, and the other person would feed him with a spoon. If he stayed awake further, then we had to stay awake as well. We were having sleepless nights. Spoon feeding was a time-consuming task. It would take nearly an hour at times. A few days later, the paediatrician gave us a nod to feed him with a bottle. The baby liked it as well. Thankfully, he was not a baby who cried too much. He was very co-operative and didn't make any fuss while feeding or burping.

I was on paternity leave for a week. Everything was going smoothly with ample allowance for Deepika to rest while we looked after the newborn. But once my leave was over, day it was becoming difficult for me to work throughout the day after having a short and fragmented sleep at nights. Both the grannies could not stay awake at once. At least one of them had to sleep because she had to take care of the household work during the day. We did not have any domestic help at that time. So it was me, along with one of them, who would take care of the baby at night. Although I didn't complain, Deepika was watchful. She asked me to sleep at night while she would herself take over my role. It had not even been ten days since the baby was born and she had immediately worn the caretaker's shoes. Her outer stitches were almost healed, but the internal ones still hurt, but she paid no heed to it.

It was now she and my mother-in-law on night duty, while mom would look after him during the day along with the household chores. In the night, Deepika would sleep as much as she could and whenever it would be time to feed the baby, her mom would prepare the milk. She would then get up, feed him and sleep again. She used to hold him in a breastfeeding position so that the baby would feel secure, wrapped in his mother's arms. Burping and anything else after that would be taken care of by her mom. With this, she was doing her job on one hand, and on the other hand, by resting in between, she was preparing herself for the next line of treatment which would start soon.

So far, the newborn was being addressed as a baby. But then, it was a time to give him a name. Usually on the twelfth day after birth, the naming ceremony is held. We, however, did not have one as it was a challenging time for us, not to forget the Covid situation. So we kept it a household affair. Only Pranali came down from Nagpur to meet him. We named him 'Swaraj'. Swaraj means self-governed, or in a way, independent. Ever since Deepika was pregnant, we had decided on the name Swaraj if it was a baby boy. I suggested this name and Deepika had agreed within a fraction of a second. She is very patriotic and fond of brave people. Both Shivaji Maharaj and Bhagat Singh used the term 'swaraj' while fighting for independence in their respective eras. So, she was very happy at the choice.

Anyway, as Swaraj was now delivered, the oncologists were supposed to take over her treatment from the gynaecologist. The entire focus would now be on taking the cancer out of her. Restrictions on treatment due to pregnancy were not present any longer. They would just wait for some time for the outer stitches to heal and then they would have a free hand to treat her as any normal cancer patient. So far the treatment had been to just stop the growth of the tumour and to keep it under control till the delivery, while trying to make it shrink. Now the focus would be to uproot it altogether.

The next step in the treatment was breast surgery. A couple of weeks after the delivery, we went to Dr. Pranjali for a checkup. It had been five weeks since Deepika had received the last chemotherapy. Hence, as suspected, the tumour had grown in size due to the gap. Not to the extent of what it was in the beginning, but yes, it had grown by half a centimetre. Also, after surgery, she was supposed to receive four more chemo sessions that included different medicines than the ones given earlier. The gap between these sessions would be three weeks, and not one week as was the case previously.

After the breast examination, Dr. Pranjali gave a second thought on the sequence of chemo and surgery. She discussed the same with Dr. Tushar as well. After carefully weighing the risks and benefits, she took a call to go for the remaining four chemo sessions first, and then surgery, followed by radiation therapy. This would serve three purposes. First, the chemotherapy would continue to shrink the tumour so the region to be removed in surgery would be smaller in size. Secondly, Deepika had just had a delivery and her stitches were not healed yet. Postponing the surgery would give her body ample time to get over from the physical trauma due to delivery, before going into another physical trauma. And third, our medical insurance, which was exhausted by now, was scheduled for renewal from the 1st of April. Hence, there was a chance that the cost of surgery, if scheduled after that, would be covered by the insurance.

Initially, from the financial point of view, I asked Dr. Pranjali if it would be possible to have the remaining chemo sessions first and then the surgery. However, not at the cost of any unwanted risk because of the swap. She said that the swap would rather be helpful for Deepika, and she would continue to assess the tumour in between the chemo gaps, if needed, they would go for surgery any time in between. Anyway, looking at the tumour's status, medically, for her it made more sense to finish the chemos first.

As per the plan then, I received a call from Dr. Jyoti a couple of days later, asking about Deepika's health. She wanted to make sure that she was fit enough to resume chemotherapy. She cascaded the prerequisite tests to be done before we could go ahead with the chemo. Just like the previous times, the diagnostic tests were supposed to be done before every chemo session. Accordingly, we got them done a day before the session, once she was okay with going ahead. By then, nearly three weeks after the delivery, she could finally sit and walk properly. She was ready to face the more challenging second innings of the cancer match which was supposed to begin the next day.

11

THE SECOND ROUND OF CHEMOTHERAPY

On the morning of 30th January 2021, we went to the hospital for the first chemo session, out of the remaining four. By now, the hospital had become a second home for us. All the concerned staff, right from nurses, doctors to the billing people, everybody knew Deepika well. It is an Indian tradition to distribute sweets whenever a child is born. So we had brought along a packet of signature sweet pedhas for all of the daycare staff to celebrate the birth of Swaraj. During the earlier sessions of chemo, the nurses used to come and ask her about how she was. A pregnant woman having chemotherapy was a rare sight for them as well. Everyone there was happy that finally the baby was delivered and that he was healthy. It was the first time since Swaraj's birth that both of us were away from him at the same time, but we were happy as he was safe with his grannies.

We settled down on her favourite bed. The rest of the set up was exactly the same. Only the medicines for the remaining four chemos were going to be different than the earlier twelve. Probably they would be stronger, as she was not pregnant anymore. A nurse inserted an intracath in her left arm to start the IV line, as it would not be allowed to be used for needle pricks after the surgery. Later, only the right arm would be used. The left one had become very hard and painful by now due to continued insertions since the last five months, and still it had to bear another three insertions in the weeks to come.

After the pre-medication, her first chemo medicine was connected to the IV line. We were amazed to see its appearance. It was a tiny bottle with an extremely dark red coloured liquid inside. It was supposed to last only for ten minutes. The next one, which was ready as well, would be for an hour. The nurse told us in advance that for a couple of days, even the colour of her urine would be red, and we need not worry. As usual, my attention went to the names of the medicines. The red one was Doxorubicin or Adriamycin and the next one was Cyclophosphamide. Together, this chemo regimen is known as AC. I would often google the names of the medicines or procedures so as to have some idea beforehend, before the doctors could tell us the details. This also helped me get my queries resolved by them, which would ultimately aim at avoiding any last-minute inconvenience, pain or stress to Deepika.

The chemo was completed within half a day. How cool that was! Even the discomfort during the administration was lesser. I thought these chemos would probably be easier to tackle. But then, Dr. Jyoti conveyed something, which gave me cold feet. Deepika was supposed to be given five filgrastim injections starting the next day.

Gosh! I have to admit I was extremely nervous. She used to be torn apart while being given a single injection during previous chemo cycles, and this time she would be getting five injections after every cycle, and that too on five consecutive days!

I asked Dr. Jyoti if it was necessary, or if we could avoid some, or if they could be given on alternate days. But her answer wasn't in favour of any of those questions. AC regimen is known to take a heavy toll on the WBC count, hence that dose of filgrastim was necessary to avoid any infection. It was conveyed by Dr. Tushar himself. I had no option but to prepare myself for the tough task of giving her injections daily. The fear was not just about that; it was also about how Deepika would cope up with it.

Once we reached home, mom told us that Swaraj had been a good boy while we were out. Though he was not even a month old, he could express his mood with a tiny smile or his body language. He was very happy seeing his mother back. Deepika just rested for the remaining day as she was dizzy. She used to sleep after every chemo for a few hours to rejuvenate herself. Apart from the injections, she was prescribed five to six different medicines to keep immediate side effects like acidity, nausea, and constipation at bay. She was also advised to have a sitz bath several times a day to avoid any external infection at the stitching area as she was immuno compromised due to the chemo.

The next day onwards, for continuous five days, I administered her the injections. For a couple of days, it was okay as two different sides were used. But then the third day onwards, the injection site would hurt terribly with the repeated jabs. Every alternate day, she got an injection on each of the sides. Bravely, she managed to bear those five painful days. But it was not just the pain of injection pricking. The back and overall body pain associated with its effect was yet to reach its peak. During the peak, which spanned for the entire next week, she was all but well. The combined effect of five injections was wreaking havoc in her body. At one point, she had fever as well. It went away eventually, but pain in the back, joints and knees persisted. For nearly two weeks after the chemo, she had to deal with the pathetic situation. There seemed to be no respite. Now we came to know why there was a three-week gap between these AC chemos. The pain of the initial twelve chemos was bad with the pregnancy being an addition. We thought that since the pregnancy was gone, she would easily be able to cope up with the remaining treatment. But just the one AC chemo was worse than the earlier twelve combined.

Deepika was not able to carry on her baby duties at night, given the unimaginable scale of body ache she was going through. Looking at her plight, I decided to take charge once again. After a discussion with my office, I changed my working hours to start from three in the afternoon, so that I could look after the feeding at night. I would sleep during the mornings after handing him over to his granny. This way Deepika could focus on her rest. She still used to wake up and sleep again while I fed him, but at least it wasn't compulsory. Many times, Swaraj would wake up during the night apart from the feeding time, so I had to pat him continuously until he fell asleep again. We would swaddle him to sleep, so I used to stay awake all night fearing he might turn over on his own and end up sleeping on his nose.

Watching something on the laptop as a distraction was still the best way to cope up with the pain for Deepika. During pregnancy, she had watched series on Chandragupta Maurya, Shivaji Maharaj and Gautam Buddha for garbh sanskar, but now she was watching her favourite series '*Yeh un dino ki baat hai*' on OTT. It was the best pain killer for her during those days. The series was based on nostalgia of the nineties. I joined her whenever I could. During those days, while I would stay awake the entire night for Swaraj, I watched this series as well, whenever I could. It took me back to my childhood memories. Due to the pandemic, pregnancy and treatment, I had not visited my hometown Akola for more than one year. I even called up my childhood best friend Sarthak a couple of times, to recall our childhood days even though we couldn't meet. That was how I dealt with the long nights.

Coming back to Deepika, things just weren't getting better. Her path so far had been full of unpleasant surprises, and the next one was around the corner. Thirteen days after the chemo, when the peak pain was over, she started experiencing some hair fall. Initially we thought it might be just a minor side effect of a preventive medicine, as the chemo so far hadn't affected hair. But then the hairfall began increasing exponentially every time she combed her hair. She liked long hair a lot, and she used to nourish and maintain hers with care. When she was younger, many of her hostel friends were fans of her long tresses and would seek her advice for hair care. But, since they began falling, she decided to cut them to half of the length, as a measure to get rid of the hairfall. But, even after that, there was no sign of stopping.

There were strands of hair everywhere in the house, no matter how many times it was swept. In a matter of three to four days, she had lost half of her hair. I remember there was a night when Swaraj was sleeping. I was just wrapping up my work on the laptop, while Deepika was combing her hair in front of me looking at the mirror. As she ran her fingers through them, a ball of hair would be entangled in her fingers. She continued for an hour. At last, what I saw was unforgettable. Half of her hair was on her head and half in her hand. It was a sight that no girl would like to see in the mirror. I could see the patches of her bald scalp.

The next morning, out of nowhere, she took Swaraj into her arms and asked me to click some photos. I was a bit surprised initially, but then I thought she was in a good mood and wanted some clicks with him, so I did it. Then she handed him over to his granny and went back to the mirror. I followed her. What she did next was the most unexpected thing I've ever seen her doing. She took my zero machine and literally shaved her head off by herself!

She realised that the chemo had taken over her hair and there was no point in trying to save them anymore. Rather than looking at the falling hair daily and getting upset in installments, she chose to shave everything off once and for all.

12

THE NEAR-DEATH EXPERIENCE

During the second AC chemo, we told Dr. Tushar that the filgrastim injections were causing more damage and pain than the chemo itself. He said that there was no way to escape them, as an infection happening at that stage could be life threatening. All he could do was to prescribe only one single injection that had a dose equivalent to five. It was known as peg-filgrastim. The most it would do was to save her injection pricks for the remaining four days which was a relief in itself. It was supposed to be taken only once on the second day of chemo. So we agreed and asked Dr. Jyoti to prescribe that in the discharge summary.

As usual, I administered her that injection on the next day and relaxed knowing the next would be only after three weeks. But the concentrated peg-filgrastim was in no mood to let us relax. It showed its effect right from day one. The overall pain of the back, muscles and joints increased by several folds compared to the earlier five. As I said earlier, the filgrastim works by forcing the bone marrow to produce more white blood cells or WBCs. As a retaliation, the bone marrow causes pain in the bones, especially in the back and joints. In layman's language, the peg-filgrastim is several times more concentrated than filgrastim with respect to its job and also with respect to the pain it causes to the body. So this one injection had brought her much more pain than the previous ones put together. Earlier, the peak was the third or fourth day and then it would gradually subside. This time, almost a week had passed and there was no sign of the pain receding, in spite of taking the pain relief medicines. Though she bore it stoically, she would moan and squirm whenever it became unbearable.

On Friday evening that week, when the pain was excruciating, Deepika was as usual trying to watch something on the laptop to distract herself. That day however, it was not helping at all. I was working on my laptop. Since seven in the evening, she started feeling a discomfort in her chest. We were habitual of muscular pain in the body so far, but that day, she was complaining of chest pain. I left my work and went to see her. I made her drink some water and asked her to relax. We knew that we couldn't do anything with respect to the pain, and that she just needed to be patient and let the time pass.

However, after some time, at around eight, she seemed to be completely in the clutches of the chest pain. I was just thinking of a way to soothe her, when suddenly she said,

"I think I'm going to die now!"

I froze. Many cancer patients are known to die mid-treatment because of some complication or the other, and both of us knew this was a possibility. However, we never thought of it, especially after Swaraj was born. Deepika's words stunned me. And as she said those words, slowly she was getting dizzy. All of a sudden, things started going out of control.

Apart from the three of us, only the grannies were present at home. Our fathers had returned to their hometowns. By this time, both of them had gathered near us. Swaraj was sleeping in his hammock in another room. I was constantly trying to speak to Deepika, but she was slowly losing consciousness. This prompted me to call the hospital and ask them for an emergency ambulance. Since her chest was hurting, I asked them to send a cardiac ambulance with a doctor on board. I came back and continuously tapped her, asking questions to keep her awake, but her eyes were half closed.

And then, looking at me, she suddenly said, "Please take care of my baby. I am leaving," and she fell unconscious!

I shouted at once, "Deepikaaa!" to try and get her to regain consciousness, but she didn't respond. I did not know what was wrong. Honestly, I was fearing the worst. Mom came to us running after hearing me scream. Both of them were weeping and continuously tapping her face to try and make her regain consciousness. She was in a sitting position and I was supporting her back when she fell unconscious. Until the ambulance arrived, we were trying different things like rubbing her palms and feet, but to no avail. All this was going on for around ten minutes. Suddenly, Swaraj also started crying in his hammock. Mom went back to him and brought him close to her. She pleaded with Deepika to open her eyes and look at him.

Maybe hearing the cries of Swaraj in her subconscious mind, she regained a bit of consciousness as I saw some motion in her fingers. When I checked, she was breathing as well, though mostly unconscious. By this time, the ambulance had arrived. There was a doctor on board. Very quickly I explained to them what had happened so far. The doctor checked her and decided to take her to the hospital. She was then shifted onto the stretcher to be taken inside the ambulance. The doctor asked me to sit in the front while he sat near her bed to start preliminary treatment en route to the hospital. For the first time in my life, I was sitting inside a speeding ambulance with its siren on, as the vehicles gave way, and red traffic signals turned green for us.

After reaching the hospital, she was taken to the emergency care ward. Dr. Tushar was informed, as her treatment was ongoing under him. As per his instructions, they started treating her. The intracath and IV line were connected again with pain relief medicines. To check exactly what had happened, they connected many probes to her, for monitoring her heartbeats on Electrocardiogram (ECG) for a few minutes. To my relief, her ECG was normal. That meant she had not suffered a heart attack or a cardiac arrest. By now, she had also regained consciousness to some extent as the heavy dose of pain relief medicine worked to reduce her pain. I asked her how she was feeling, and once again she asked me where Swaraj was. I told her what had happened and how she came to be at the hospital.

As a precautionary measure, they did a chest X-ray to rule out anything abnormal. The X-ray was fine. After they were done with the tests, the doctor explained to me that she was in extreme pain because of the chemo. Maybe due to her sitting posture, the muscles near the heart were strained and that's how she had stiffness and pain there. It was not the heart itself, but the muscles around it that were paining. She was already exhausted with the body pain as well, and when all that cumulative pain went beyond her tolerance limit, she fell unconscious. She was perfectly fine with respect to the health of her heart. This explanation had certainly brought me some respite.

Around half past ten, the doctor asked her how she was feeling and if she needed to rest a little while longer. She was much better by now as the medicines had acted swiftly. She wanted to leave as she was missing Swaraj. The doctor gave us a prescription with changed medicine to suit her scale of pain. He asked her to take it immediately whenever she started feeling that the pain was going beyond control, so that such episodes didn't recur in the future. After coming back, she took Swaraj into her arms and hugged him. She remembered what she said before falling unconscious.

"You must say 'sorry'. And promise me you will never say that ever again," I said to her.

She said, "Sorry, I won't." And she hugged our son tightly.

By this time, Jayesh and Kajal had arrived from Mumbai, after my mother-in-law called them and told them what had happened. We finally had our dinner late at night. While getting ready for bed, I narrated to her how things had gone out of hand all of a sudden, while she had dealt with and successfully handled even worse kinds of pain in the past. Probably she was suffering from postpartum depression to some extent as well. It is something that many women suffer after delivery without even knowing that they are suffering from it. A woman's body goes through a lot of hormonal changes after delivery. There is a sudden feeling of emptiness. Not just the body, even the routine life changes completely. The entire daily routine moves only around the baby. The duties, the responsibilities and the priorities change too, contributing to postpartum depression.

Unknowingly, even I was one of the contributors. During her pregnancy, I had been with her continuously, but now, I was not able to dedicate much of my time to her. After being awake at night, I used to sleep the entire mornings, and then from three in the afternoon to half past eleven in the night, I'd work. Hence, there was a disconnect between us. She had lost her precious hair on top of that. Because of all these factors, she was depressed. And to add to it, the chemo and filgrastim injection made things worse. I realised that somewhere in the game of office-office, I had taken her courage for granted. I promised her that from then onwards, I would be with her throughout the day for as long as I could. She was a tough warrior and healthy Swaraj was proof of that. I just reminded her of her own power and asked her not to ever give up again. One had to hold on while undergoing such a lengthy and agonising treatment. It was difficult, but not impossible as Deepika herself was proving day after day.

We were very happy after the discussion. After all, it had been a long time since we had spent more than an hour together in one go. She was once again ready to face the challenges head on.

13

TRANSITION FROM CHEMO TO SURGERY

After the near-death experience, we were extremely cautious and monitored the pain closely. Once we were done with the next chemotherapy in the second week of March, especially after the peg-filgrastim injection, we kept a careful eye on the escalating pain. The required medicines were ready too. As they say, once bitten twice shy. There couldn't be a recurrence of the episode. Nearly six days after the chemo, she nearly reached the limit when it was going beyond tolerance. This time the pain was centered in the back. She immediately took the new medicine and within a couple of hours she was, not out of it I would say, but the pain came down to a bearable limit.

It was almost time for the chemotherapy to be over. It would soon be time for the next step – surgery. The fourth and final chemo session was scheduled for the 3rd of April, and ten days after that, Dr. Pranjali planned a surgery to remove the residual tumour. Now as far as the surgery goes, it was not supposed to be just a surgery. There was something else associated with it that would be irreversible, and it was going to be a part of Deepika's life forever.

Whenever any person suffers from breast cancer, there is a possibility that it might have further spread to the lymph nodes, and in turn, to other parts of the body. Lymph nodes are multiple tiny bean shaped organs present all over the body, tasked to drain the lymphatic fluid or leaked fluid of the body, filter it and empty it back to the bloodstream. The scale of the spread of cancer is different for different people and depends on how late it was diagnosed.

The nodes where the breast cancer cells are most likely to have spread are the axillary lymph nodes which are situated in the underarms. To stop the spread of cancer, in most of the cases, the surgeons remove the axillary lymph nodes. In Deepika's case too, they were supposed to be removed. It is a different surgery known as axillary lymph node dissection and it was to be done in the same sitting as the breast surgery. Since the lymph nodes cannot be replaced, there is a constant risk of arm swelling, known as lymphedema, for a lifetime. But then, if we weigh the risks and benefits, removing the lymph nodes makes more sense than to let them be there and risk the cancer from recurring. For lymphedema management, there are some exercises and precautions that the patient has to follow for a lifetime.

Dr. Pranjali explained all of the above in that meeting. We were also curious to know what was to be done after the surgery and more details about the rest of the treatment. As usual, she replied with her signature statement, "Let us go step by step." She said that first the surgery would be performed and then the rest of the issues would be addressed in accordance to Deepika's response and situation at that time. She had been the captain of this multidisciplinary treatment team for the last seven months and this step-by-step approach was the best thing she followed. She would divide everything into smaller targets, and would take a decision based on real time situation rather than pre-deciding the entire regimen beforehand. Her approach also helped us take up one challenge at a time, aiming towards Deepika's recovery systematically.

Before we could go for the surgery, some tests had to be done. Apart from the usual pathology tests, there was one very important test known as PET scan. This test is used to determine the status of an existing tumour and to check if it had metastasized, meaning if it had spread to the other organs of the body. It is similar to a CT scan, but uses a different technology, which is more accurate with respect to the diagnosis of the spread of cancer.

There were just a couple of weeks remaining for Deepika's surgery, but the concept of lymph node removal was bothering me a lot. I was just curious to ascertain whether its side-effects would seriously bother her for the rest of her life. I did a lot of googling around it. I even called up Aditi for the same. Aditi was Pratique's friend, but ever since we met her and her hubby Nikhil at his engagement, they had become our friends too. I remember Aditi had told us that her sister too had undergone breast cancer surgery a few years ago. I asked her for her sister's number. I spoke to her sister right then, and asked her about her experience. She too had undergone lymph node removal during the surgery. She said that lymph node removal certainly brought in some limitations, but not to the extent that one won't be able to live a normal life. I also got a couple of other breast cancer survivors' contacts from her, who had undergone the same surgery. I spoke to them, and they too were living a normal life with respect to the operated arm just by following some precautions in day-to-day life. I was relieved to some extent after speaking with them.

After the last chemo session on Saturday, the 3rd of April, it was time to say goodbye to the daycare facility, to Dr. Jyoti and to Dr. Tushar. She had already undergone sixteen chemo sessions so far. Dr. Tushar in his last visit lauded Deepika's great show of patience and endurance during the treatment under him. Dr. Pranjali used to brief him after every tumour assessment, and he too was happy with the response. After all the efforts of the previous eight months, he had been successful in bringing her cancer tumour to a stage where it was possible to have lumpectomy rather than a more aggressive mastectomy.

The last chemo was over, but the last peg-filgrastim injection was still pending. I was happy that I wouldn't have to inflict the cruelty ever again. It was the twentieth and the last time she was supposed to be injected. On the evening of Monday, I did it and then I was free. She was ready to face a week of agony one last time. The pain medicines were ready and handy. While she was dealing with her suffering, there was another unpleasant surprise. When you already have a cancer patient at home, you would always want others to be healthy to look after that person. But then, it was my turn to fall ill.

On the evening of Tuesday, I started feeling a sore throat, had a runny nose and fever. The second wave of Coronavirus led by the delta variant was spreading havoc all over India and Pune was one of the worst hit cities. Pratique and Vishal were already Covid positive. Although I hadn't met them for a while, my symptoms made me suspect I could be Covid positive as well. I thought probably during her chemo session, I might have contracted the infection from someone in the hospital. I had no option, but to isolate myself in a separate room as Deepika was already immuno compromised and Swaraj was just three months old. We couldn't afford to delay her surgery on account of me being Covid positive, as the tumour, in that case, would also grow further in the absence of chemo.

On top of everything, apart from the three of us, it was just mom who was at home. Dad was in our hometown. Deepika's parents had gone to Mumbai to look after Jayesh and Kajal, both of whom were Covid positive. They couldn't come back for fifteen days at least. Looking at the situation, Deepika decided to take a charge once again. I wonder how she tolerated her pain during the peak time and still looked after Swaraj single-handedly, while Mom took care of the cooking and household activities. Sitting helpless in an isolated room, I immediately called up Dad and asked him to come back to Pune taking the very first means of transport that he would get. Even Pranali was planning to come down from Nagpur at the time of surgery. I called her up, and asked her to leave for Pune along with Dad right away without waiting further.

It had been three days since I had been locked up. Both the leading ladies were putting up a good partnership in spite of the adverse conditions, to successfully bat for Swaraj. He was accustomed to his father handling him. But since I was not there, he used to look for me here and there. And when he used to pass by my room with his granny, he used to look at me as if asking me to take him in my arms. I, however, was helpless.

I had already submitted my sample for the Covid test, but had not yet received the report. Those days, during the second wave, an RTPCR report would take around two to three days to be out. Finally, when on Friday I received the report, it was negative! It was just a normal cold, which anyway had subsided by then. I immediately had a bath and the first thing that I did was to cuddle my baby. Had my report been positive, I would be barred from accompanying Deepika during her hospitalisation for the surgery, which was the most crucial step in her treatment. I was greatly relieved. The pandemic was playing hide and seek with us. At both the times, both our reports were negative and still we had to deal with some serious inconvenience.

The next day, we went to the hospital for a PET scan. It took around four hours for the scan to get completed. PET scan involves injecting the patient with some radioactive drug, which is used to trace normal and abnormal activities in the body, and hence to find out the spread of cancer. For this reason, Deepika was not supposed to go near Swaraj for at least twelve hours after the test, till the radioactive material was flushed out of the body. On Monday, she was supposed to be admitted for the surgery and the PET scan report would also be out that morning. I was not ready to wait till then, as I was very anxious to know whether the cancer had reached other parts of the body. I requested the PET scan specialist to release the report if it would be ready by the end of that day itself.

Finally, I collected the reports the same evening. As usual, I could not refrain from opening and reading the report at the collection counter itself, before I sent it to the doctor. It said,

'No Metastasis.'

So the cancer had not spread to the other organs. I was so relieved to read those words. After coming back home, I sent the report to Dr. Pranjali and she confirmed that there was no metastasis. This report was very important for her from the surgical point of view, as it accurately described the nature, location and size of the tumour.

While speaking with her, I once again discussed the need for removal of the lymph nodes and its side effects later in life. She told me that it was imperative to remove them or else we would risk her life by letting the suspected carriers bring back cancer in the future. She, however, told me about the procedure named Axillary Reverse Mapping that she was going to do. It involved injecting a blue dye in the underarm area, because of which the lymphatic carrier nodes, draining the dye, become visible during the surgery. She said she would remove only those many nodes which seemed to be the carriers, and keep the others intact. This explanation from Dr. Pranjali helped me gain confidence in the procedure, which was clearly unavoidable.

The next day which was Sunday, we got Deepika's Covid test done beforehand. It was mandatory for hospitalisation. It was the fourth time she was taking the test during this treatment. But this time it was just a prerequisite, and it turned out negative as well. Swaraj would be staying with his grandparents for the next four days, as both of us would be staying at the hospital. We were relaxed, as he was very co-operative and familiar with his grandparents. In addition, Pranali would be helping them, and doing the runs to and fro between home and the hospital.

14

REMOVAL OF TUMOUR AND LYMPH NODES

On Monday evening, we were supposed to get Deepika admitted for the planned surgery. Not sure if there was some connection between the rain and her milestones of treatment, but whenever something major was about to happen, it would rain. On Monday evening too, it was raining when we both left for the hospital. While Deepika was waiting at the lounge, I was completing the admission formalities, when I heard someone there asking me how Deepika was doing? I just turned around to see Dr. Prajakta from the gynaecology department. We spoke for a minute. I felt happy that she remembered Deepika in spite of handling a large number of patients daily. But this time she was herself a patient. She was Covid positive and had come to get herself admitted. It was the peak of the second wave in Pune with all the hospitals running short of beds. The next day onwards, another total lockdown was about to start.

Once inside our room, and till the time the pre-procedure started, we relaxed as if we were staying in a hotel room. I suppose we had lost the fear of hospitalisation by then. We ordered our favourite food while watching TV. Those days, we used to watch the show '*Indian Idol*'. After we finished dinner and one of its episodes, a couple of nurses came in to insert an intracath into her arm. Now that time, and from there on, only her right arm was supposed to be used for any needle prick. The next morning, along with surgery, her left axillary lymph nodes would be removed, and once done with that, no needle prick would be allowed on that arm for a lifetime.

An anaesthesiologist came in to take the case history and to make sure she did not have any allergy to the anaesthesia. She was supposed to be under general anaesthesia, or complete unconsciousness throughout the surgery. He also made us sign the consent form for the surgery. She was not allowed to eat or drink anything after midnight. The IV fluids had been started by then, which would take care of her energy needs. She needed to sleep well as her surgery had been planned for the next morning at 8 a.m.

13th April 2021

She was shifted to the operation theatre at around 07:30 a.m. I wished her all the best, just before she was being taken inside. While coming out, I saw Dr. Pranjali going in. She stopped for a while to have a word with me before proceeding. Everything was already clear to me after our call the day before. I just asked her how much time it would take. She said that the entire procedure would take around three to four hours. Once she went in, I came back to the room and had my breakfast. I continuously prayed that Deepika was alright and everything was going on without any issue.

Pranali came in at 9 a.m. She told me that Swaraj was fine at home. Being a doctor, I asked her to stay with me so that she could speak with Dr. Pranjali in medical terms and understand the procedure better whenever she would be out. Around 11:30 a.m. both of us went down outside the OT. The guard told me that the procedure was still going on and the doctors had not come out yet.

At 01:30 p.m., after almost six hours now, I saw Dr. Pranjali coming out with her assistant surgeon. It had taken them much longer than the projected time. I was just hoping that everything had gone well. Looking at her coming out, Pranali and I stepped forward to meet her. She said everything had gone as per the plan, and just that they needed to additionally do the rotational flap which had taken time. She went on to tell us in detail about the surgical procedures done.

It was basically a breast surgery, plus lymph node removal, plus the rotational flap which is a plastic surgery to restore the shape of breast after the removal of the tumour. Earlier I thought it would only be the removal of tumour and then the lining would be stitched. But that was not all. It was not as easy as it sounded. The doctor had to remove the entire area or sector where the cancer was present along with a one to two centimetre-thick layer of healthy tissues surrounding the tumour. This was done to ensure that the cancer tumour remained well encapsulated within the healthy tissues after the removal. Even if one cancer cell was exposed to the rest of the healthy area, then there would be a chance that it would further multiply and again bring back the cancer later in life. Hence the careful carving and removal of the area was done. The earlier known fibroadenoma was also removed within the same mass.

Now when such a big amount of mass was removed from the breast, the remaining couldn't be stitched as it is, else there would be a big visible depression at the site. In order to make it a breast shape again, plastic surgery known as rotational flap was done. To understand it in layman's terms, one can imagine that, if a sector from a circle is removed, then in order to make it a near-circle again, one of the edges of the sector is anchored at its place, and the remaining circle is rotated around the center to pull the other edge inwards. Both the edges are then joined with stitches, to close the gap. In Deepika's case, since the rotational flap was done to restore the aesthetics, she had a long circular cut line all along, which needed a large number of stitches too. At the bottom, there were literally stapler pins inserted all along the cut line, to keep the two sides together firmly till they healed and became one single body.

That was only the breast surgery. The next was lymph nodes removal. Dr. Pranjali made an incision in the underarm to access the lymph nodes area, and dissected or removed the nodes there after completing the axillary reverse mapping. There were drain tubes inserted at both the sites of surgery

– breast cut line and underarm cut line, to let the fluid drain out till the surgical cuts healed and the fluid draining stopped. The drain tubes were supposed to be removed after a couple of weeks. Honestly, it takes some serious guts to perform such a procedure with utmost accuracy. All thanks to Dr. Pranjali who had uprooted and thrown the cancer out of Deepika's body and ensured that it would have minimal chances of returning by removing the axillary lymph nodes.

So that was all about the procedure. Now, after going through such a tedious and complicated surgery, with dozens of stitches once again, my heart started fearing for the immense amount of pain that Deepika was going to suffer, once she would wake up from the anaesthesia. She was shifted back to the room at around 04:00 p.m. after spending a couple of hours under observation in the recovery ward beside the OT. She was half awake and spoke a couple of words with me. The pain relief medicines were already going in through her IV line. It was good to have her back and I prayed that she wouldn't suffer.

After 06:00 p.m., she was allowed to start having fluids, starting with water. But she was too nauseated to have anything. The effect of the anaesthesia had brought severe nausea to her. It was expected. From the very night when the effect of the anaesthesia vanished, she started feeling the pain in her entire left side. She was complaining of a heavy pain, especially in her underarm. It was a movable part, so it would hurt even if there was slightest of the movement. The armpit is a very sensitive part anyway, and she had a long surgical cut right there.

Due to the surgery, it was very challenging to hold her arms while lifting her in order to make her sit or sleep in different positions. Both her arms were swollen to double their size. This swelling was expected and it would go away soon. However, the swelling on the left arm where lymph nodes were removed was supposed to remain for a few weeks till the body adjusted with the condition. Some new channels for drainage would be automatically created by then, but they wouldn't be having the capability of lymph nodes. She would have to do draining exercises of her operated arm daily for a lifetime, in order to help drain the lymphatic fluid from arm, and to avoid swelling. But for a couple of days, she was not supposed to lift her left arm above ninety degrees.

Around 09:00 p.m., I tried to feed her some food as both her hands were inactive at that moment. The left arm had been operated on, and there was an intracath in the right one. She ate a few bites, but soon she started feeling nauseous again. I called a nurse to let her know that she was not able to eat. I also needed to make her sit by lifting her. It was not possible for me alone as I might hurt her while trying to do that. I asked the nurse to help me make her sit up. The moment she sat, she threw up every morsel inside her stomach. It was entirely blue in colour. I asked the doctor, and she said there was nothing to worry about. Deepika's body fluids would remain blue for a couple of days because of the blue dye she had been injected with, before the lymph node surgery. After some time, I tried to make her eat again, but the same thing happened. The nurse was very kind to stay there and help me while she puked. She even arranged a couple of containers, to try and avoid staining the clothes and bed linen. That night Deepika couldn't eat or drink at all.

14th April 2021

The next morning, Dr. Pranjali came in for a checkup. She checked if all of Deepika's surgical wounds were healing, and saw the quantity of the drain accumulated inside the container. Initially it was around 120 ml a day, which was supposed to gradually come down in a couple of weeks. She made her do some basic movements of the operated arm. We also got her up and let her walk for a few minutes. There was still terrible pain at the surgical sites, but Deepika was somehow bearing it with the help of painkillers. Gradually the nausea also subsided and she could eat some juice and some soft solid food.

Dr. Pranjali asked me to arrange a specific type of sportswear inners for her, which she was supposed to wear for a month at least, to firmly hold the operated breast till the surgical wounds healed properly. This was another challenge as everything was shut due to the second wave of Covid. Even online orders were not being taken. I asked Pranali to try and arrange it from outside by visiting the closed stores in person and calling the numbers mentioned on storefronts, so that at least somebody would pick up and open the store for five minutes. After a lot of phone calls, she managed to arrange one a couple of days later.

On the same evening of fourteenth, Deepika complained about unbearable pain in underarm and the surgical sites.

Although pain relief medicine was being administered to her through the IV line, it was not sufficient to keep it under bearable limit. With great difficulty, she managed to have dinner, but the pain was in no mood to subside. On the contrary, it began to escalate. She said it was feeling like a continuous knife stabbing. As I feared, the magnitude of this pain was breaking the records of previous painful episodes from chemotherapy. The intensity was such that she started moaning and tears began streaming down her face. She could tolerate a great deal of pain as I and all her doctors had already seen. But this pain was challenging the limits of her endurance.

I rushed to the nursing station and asked them to have a look. It was 9:00 p.m. A doctor came in a couple of minutes. She was surprised, as the pain should have been bearable because of the medicines. After an examination, she found that the medicines were not going into her body as the intracath was out. This meant she was no longer receiving the medicines from the IV line. This was the reason her pain had increased by several folds. Since the painkillers were not reaching her, the surgical cuts must have truly felt like knife stabs. Poor Deepika!

While she was grabbed in the clutches of survival challenging pain, there was an urgent need to put in another intracath in her arm to restart the painkillers. But again, like dozens of previous challenges she had faced, one more emerged. Her arm was swollen and no nurse was successful in finding the vein despite trying at several places. An anaesthesiologist was called in to do the tough task. Usually, anaesthesiologists are experts in inserting the IV catheter or intracath in the difficult to find veins. The same anesthesiologist who was present during her surgery was to arrive in five minutes. But even after twenty minutes, there was no sign of him. I went out to the nursing station and they said he was on the same floor, busy with another patient, but he would come soon.

I had no option, but to wait. Deepika's pain was aggravating with every passing minute. Five minutes later, I saw him doing some paperwork at the counter. I requested him to come with me right away, but he seemed unfazed. Finally, after ten minutes, he arrived in our room with a nurse. He too tried locating a vein, but couldn't succeed, as her arm was terribly swollen. He said that he would give it a last try or else they would have to look for other options. I am not sure what those 'other options' were. Somewhere near the front of the elbow, he located a small vein and gave it a last try. The last attempt is something that has always worked for Deepika, and this time too, it worked. He was successful in inserting it in the very last attempt.

Immediately after the intracath insertion, the nurse started the IV line with the pain relief medicine. The nurses left, but she was still not out of pain.

"I should have died instead of this torture of hell!" she cried at one point.

It was the first time I heard those words from her in the course of the entire treatment so far. She was frustrated to the power infinity. Till the pain subsided, I tried to distract her by talking to her about random stuff, but to no avail. That was the second toughest time for me after the near-death experience of February. This experience was nevertheless, nothing short of that. Gradually, in a couple of hours, her pain came down within the bearable limit, and she could finally sleep. When we had settled in the hospital as if checking in a hotel a couple of days ago, neither of us thought that the surgery would be such a big thing to deal with.

15th April 2021

Deepika was much better the next morning. The swelling in the right arm had also reduced. She could now get up by herself and walk. Dr. Pranjali sent her a bag to carry the drain container. It was very convenient for her to walk with the bag on her shoulder. The drain output was nearly hundred milliliters per day. It was supposed to be under thirty ml for the removal of the drain tubes. It would take anywhere from two to three weeks. Till then she was supposed to have those inserted at the surgical sites, and carry the bag along wherever she went.

After all the struggle with the post-operative pain for the past two days, finally she seemed okay, bearing the rest of it. She could at least stand, walk, eat, and speak normally, although the parts operated upon still hurt. She was now back in control of herself, which had been taken away by adverse conditions for a couple of days, especially the episode of the previous evening.

It was not just the recovery that made her cheerful. There was something else which quadrupled her happiness. Swaraj arrived in our room along with his grandparents. It was an out of the world feeling. Both of us met our junior self after three long days. He looked overjoyed on seeing his mother. Although he hadn't bothered his grandparents too much all these days, the joy of meeting his mother was clearly visible on his face. His cooperation was a big factor in helping us tackle the varied situations without having to worry about him.

In the evening, Deepika walked out of the room after two days. There was a garden on the same floor of the hospital. We walked around in the garden for half an hour, after which she felt really good. The next day, Dr. Pranjali checked the surgical wounds and hand movement again. She was happy with the overall response of the treatment during the past four days and initiated Deepika's discharge. It was time to go home with certain precautions. Sanitation care for the stitches and the drain tube area was the most important, as her immunity was compromised due to the chemo and it would take a few more months for it to increase. She was advised to strictly stay clear of infections. Also, her drain discharge was to be measured every day. Once her wounds healed and the bandages were off, she was supposed to undergo radiation therapy, which was the next and the final leg of treatment.

15

RADIATION THERAPY AND REHABILITATION

With the surgery completed, the toughest part of Deepika's treatment was over. It was the end of chemo therapy, filgrastim injections and surgery. Even the diagnostic part was over. While performing surgery, it was taken care that the tumour, after removal, was well encapsulated within the healthy tissues, and that not even a single fragment of it remained inside the body. But still, as a precautionary measure, the areas of surgery and lymph nodes were supposed to receive radiation therapy. Radiations target and kill the cancer cells by destroying their DNA and hence killing them or stopping their multiplication. In Deepika's case, since the tumour was already surgically removed, radiation therapy was going to be a postoperative prevention to stop the cancer from coming back in the future.

For radiation to begin, her wounds were supposed to heal first, and she had to be able to raise and hold her operated arm straight up. To help with the arm exercise part, Dr. Pranjali referred us to a cancer rehabilitation physiotherapist or oncophysiotherapist, Dr. Sharada. She had planned to start the targeted arm exercises right after a week. The key was – the sooner you start, the better is the regaining of movement. As time passes, it becomes very difficult to regain the flexibility, and the movement of the arm gets restricted forever. Dr. Sharada was Covid positive at that time, but kind enough to ensure that Deepika started her exercises within time by doing a couple of video sessions with her. Right from the basic exercises to the cyclic ones, she got all of them done well within time. Day by day, slowly and steadily, Deepika regained the movement of her left arm, and soon it was almost equal to that of the right one.

The drain tubes were a bit of a hurdle during the exercises as the site used to pain a lot while moving the arm. Dr. Sharada however, advised her to continue the pain medicine to manage it, and carry on doing the exercises for a bigger gain. Three weeks after the surgery, in the first week of May, her drain tubes were taken off at last as the discharge dropped below thirty ml. The cut lines had healed externally. The staple pins were also removed along with the drain tubes. There was no foreign material attached to the surgical sites anymore.

On the same day, when her drain tubes were removed, we met Dr. Vikas, who is a radiation oncologist at the same hospital. Dr. Pranjali, as per her step-by-step approach, referred us to him. He was about to take over the treatment from her. It was the last leg. He explained to us the plan for the radiation therapy. It would consist of twenty sessions. One session every day from Monday to Friday. Saturday and Sunday would be off. So, the entire therapy was supposed to last for four weeks, or roughly a month. Each session would be just ten minutes long, and it would consist of exposing all of the affected area to radiation for five minutes under the machine. The plan was to administer her the radiation in small and regular doses. Day by day, the cancer cells, if present, would start breaking and ultimately die and flushed out of the body by the end of the therapy.

There was a need of carefully executing the radiation dosage, as her heart was also on the same side. If the heart is exposed to consistent radiation, it could lead to cardiac injury and severe side effects later in life. Hence, to restrict the dose to the heart and optimize the treatment, the breathing stop and start technique was supposed to be followed. In this technique, during those five minutes, Deepika was supposed to breathe only from her mouth inside a tube. She had to do the cycles of inhaling and holding her breath for a few seconds and then exhaling and inhaling again. The radiation would also stop and start depending on her breathing. Basically, when air is inhaled, the heart contracts and moves inboard, hence moves away from the area of radiation exposure. When the breath is released, heart gets relaxed and again expands outboard. Radiation doses were supposed to be administered only when she would be inhaling and holding her breath, and while exhaling, it would be off.

There were still a couple of days for the radiation therapy to start. Deepika was given a tube-like instrument to carry at home for practicing the breathing start and stop technique. She had been practicing yoga and pranayama since her childhood, hence she was already a pro in this technique. Since day one itself, she could very well hold her breath and finish the session quickly. It used to be a matter of going in and coming out in just five to ten minutes, but we had to visit the hospital daily. Arm movement wise, she had to hold it straight up during the radiation session. Initially, she had a bit of trouble raising it fully for a few days, but then after doing the exercises prescribed by Dr. Sharada, she achieved full movement of her arm.

For the first two weeks, radiation did not bring any pain or inconvenience. But then, from the third week, she started feeling a burning sensation in the skin exposed to it. After all, radiation indeed induces a slow burning of the cells. As a side-effect, even healthy cells had to pay the price. But after the treatment, they regenerate. The outer layer of her skin, which was directly exposed, started to burn and ultimately peel off day after day. Dr. Vikas said that it was totally normal for a person getting radiation therapy. He requested her to bear with it and that he would prescribe medicines later for the skin to grow back.

Meanwhile, the Government of India widened the age window for Covid vaccination from the 1st of May. Everyone above eighteen years of age was now eligible to take the vaccine. However, there was a heavy rush for the registrations online, as initially the number of available doses was limited and everybody was in a hurry to get vaccinated. I was also trying from day one to get Deepika vaccinated. She was already immuno compromised, hence I wanted to get her vaccinated against Covid as soon as I could. I confirmed from all of the doctors that she could receive the vaccine safely. To get her a slot, I would give it a try every day, but as soon as the online window opened, the website would get crashed. Finally, in the last week of May, I managed to book a slot and got her vaccinated with the first dose.

Eventually, on the 4th of June, her treatment was complete. After all of the suffering, she could finally breathe freely. It was time to say goodbye to the hospital – our second home for all these months. Even after the treatment, during rehabilitation, she would suffer from back and joint pain, collectively induced by chemotherapy and pregnancy. This pain, as the doctors said, would go away gradually in a few months as the body rejuvenated itself. Though we were happy that the treatment was over, parenting was a challenging task for us for the next few months, especially because of her continuous body pain.

There came a time when our parents had to go back to the hometown because of unavoidable reasons, and it was just the two of us taking care of Swaraj. He was six months old and it had been just a month since Deepika had completed her treatment. On the one hand, it was the time to switch Swaraj from milk to solid food, and on the other, Deepika's body pain was still severe and she couldn't look after Swaraj by herself, especially taking care of his meals. Being a dietician, she was very particular about his diet. As she couldn't feed him mother's milk, making sure she cooked for him and that he ate a healthy diet was her topmost priority, even above her own recovery and rest.

She would cook for the three of us while I would work during the day. I remember there were instances when, because of meetings, I could not take out any time to look after Swaraj while she would be cooking. I still don't know how she managed everything on her own. Once I'd get free, I'd often find her holding him in one hand and cooking with another. People use phrases like 'Nothing is impossible', 'Where there is a will there's a way', 'Never say die', and so on; but I used to watch these phrases come alive often looking at her.

Deepika, because of her low immunity, suffered from a medical condition known as herpes zoster in September. It is a condition where you have painful blisters on one side of your upper body. This is the same virus that causes chickenpox in kids. It is highly contagious so she was not allowed to touch Swaraj for a week, until she got better. But then, as the saying goes, those who scale mountains do not fear hillocks. We managed to overcome that situation as well.

With every passing month, Deepika was getting better with respect to the pain. Our lives had started coming back on track. Time is the best healer. With time, we tend to forget everything and move on. But I did not want her struggle to be forgotten. After all, it was a miraculous survival story. I made up my mind to pen down her tale and started writing this book. I am not a seasoned writer, but my will to narrate her story to the world gave me enough dose of motivation to carry on writing. For more than six months most of my time, except for office hours, was spent on writing. Deepika, although in her recovery phase, would always cooperate by looking after Swaraj on her own.

I remember Dr. Vikas, during our interaction on the last day of treatment, said that Deepika will be an inspiration to many women who are fearful about cancer to such an extent that they don't even go for a checkup even if they notice something unusual. He said that many women shy away from checkups and keep their lumps a secret. He saw many of them coming to the hospital at the last stage when their cancer is spread beyond the scope of treatment. There is a need to spread awareness about cancer in India, especially in the rural areas, where discussing breast cancer or even the breast, is considered a taboo. Cancer is something that can happen to any individual, healthy or unhealthy. But it is definitely not something to fear, if one has awareness about it. Medical science has advanced a lot and cancer is not as deadly as it used to be earlier. If diagnosed at an early stage, it can be very well managed and won't be a big thing to deal with. Reporting anything abnormal to the doctor as soon as possible and having periodic checkups is the key.

Deepika's journey of fighting and winning the battle against cancer during her pregnancy was incomparable. Her positivity, patience, endurance and will-power not only managed to kick the cancer off, but she also delivered a healthy child during the treatment. If I sit back and analyse the entire last one year, every good thing that happened to her was at the brink of collapse. Her cancer was diagnosed just at the optimum time when neither could we abort the child nor delay the treatment. But, in the end, both childbirth and cancer treatment were successful. Even if destiny made her suffer, it did not let her suffer for life by aborting her baby.

Life is full of surprises, good or bad. But each surprise teaches us a lesson and makes us a better and stronger person. When the two of us were sitting on that rock facing the mighty Mount Kanchenjunga in February 2020 and enjoying the *haseen waadiyaan* and *khula aasmaan*, little did we have an idea of what destiny had on offer for us in a few months. If I think of what did Deepika get in return for her suffering, there is just one answer – Swaraj.